A
Soldiers Story
Remembered...

Family, Service and Legacy

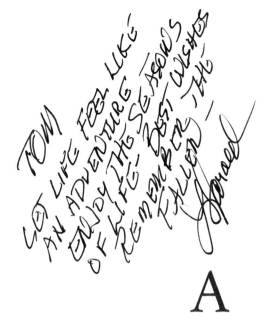

TOM!
GOT LIFE FEEL LIKE
AN ADVENTURE
ENJOY THE SEASONS
OF LIFE. BEST WISHES
REMEMBER THE
FALLEN!
Harold

THANK YOU

A
Soldiers Story
Remembered...

Family, Service and Legacy

THE DEPTHS OF CHALLENGES

Harold L. Maples

MILL CITY PRESS

Mill City Press, Inc.
2301 Lucien Way #415
Maitland, FL 32751
407.339.4217
www.millcitypress.net

Paperback ISBN-13: 978-1-66288-084-1
Ebook ISBN-13: 978-1-66288-085-8

This book is dedicated to the families of fallen heroes, men and women who provided service to their country and answered a call greater than themselves to defend our country. This is a tribute to the men and women of the military acting with a sense of purpose to defend freedom and becoming casualties of war.

ABOUT THE COVER—LIFE AND DEATH MERGE

Life and death merge. We are connected to any and all life and death. As long as living and dying things exist, life and death exist. This means you experience a spiritual and an emotional connection. "For God so loved the world, that he gave His only begotten Son, that whosoever believeth in Him should not perish, but have everlasting life" (John 3:16).

Arm in arm, side by side, this picture became a unique double exposure. A portrait of Korea—The Forgotten War— taken during the Korean War on the rim of the Punch Bowl of army buddies Harold Maples and Howard Hinkle. No soldier left behind; a soldier's life and death merge. Facing death is inevitable, as they serve their country each and every day. Is this luck or fate? Those who make it home fade into the mainstream of American life while keeping memories to themselves. It is a shame that most of the veterans who died serving in Korea have been forgotten.

There are memories, yes, of Fort Jackson, Fort Lewis, and the pipeline to the Far East: Camp Drake, Pusan, Route North, as we remember a group of former civilians who came to war to do a job to defend freedom. Our unit was on Heartbreak and Sandbag Castle near Satae-ri, near the 38th parallel, a dividing line where it all began and ended. As soldiers, we would quickly learn that our journey would completely change our lives forever, creating a new approach to life and death. A memorial to the fallen, honoring the countless soldiers who have died on the field of battle and those still placing their lives before their own for our freedom. A reflection of memories that all veterans share; a meaningful reminder that honors our comrades—many of whom have not been accounted for. The fallen heroes become mindful through the photo imagery and war experiences for a cause greater than self. Perhaps you may glean a similar reaction. Remember the fallen—freedom is not free.

TABLE OF CONTENTS

FOREWORD

At the age of twenty-two, Harold was inducted into the United States Army in October 1952. He completed his basic training at Fort Jackson, South Carolina, before being pipelined to the Far East command to Service Company 224th Infantry Regiment of the 40th Sun Burst Division. He was then assigned to Graves Registration Section in an area commonly known geographically as the Punch Bowl. He had no idea what his future held or what he was getting into—a typical army assignment.

In the war zone, there is a view of war from ground level that remains with all veterans. There is that personal view of what you see and the emotions that surface. You see the citizens of the country, old folks and young children, many being orphaned by the ravages of war. You note the topography and weather of the country, destroyed cities, and refugee villages. A soldier seeks out creative comforts in a bunker or field tent after slogging through mud, snow, rain, and extreme heat. Traveling over narrow mountainous roads and high terrain, a soldier develops eerie feelings. If you happen to be one of the lucky ones and return home, you can look up into a dark, clear, starry sky and reflect on your experience. Hard to forget?

Snowy Korea Terrain 1952–1954

Were we fighting the growth of Communism or were we only one of President Harry Truman's toy soldiers and his desire to provide police action at the cost of lives? Don't win; just delay action. Were the sacrifices in Korea worth it; to develop a line approximately two and a half miles wide and 155 miles long to shield South Korea from North Korea?

"To the men of the 40th, you came to the war once again as civilian soldiers and have once again proven that bankers, clerks, school teachers, and students, even though not totally prepared, are always ready to defend freedom" (Brigadier General Omar Nelson).

PREFACE

The manuscript for this writing was commenced by my wife, Phyllis, by arranging and cataloging countless photos and comments from my military service in Korea. The manuscript was finalized by the relentless effort of our daughter, Karen, along with insight from our son, Lloyd, and my granddaughters, Samantha and Kelly. We persevere to carry on the legacy of Korean War Veterans.

A soldier is taught and trained to stand together, cover each other's backs and to stand firm, enduring difficulties and hardships. The following is a soldier's descriptive image as found in the scripture Ecclesiastes:

A Time to Judge Every Deed
Ecclesiastes 3:1–8

Verse 1: To everything there is a season and a time to every purpose under the heaven;

Verse 2: a time to be born, and a time to die; a time to plant, and a time to pluck up what is planted;

Verse 3: a time to kill, and a time to heal; a time to break down, and a time to build up;

Verse 4: a time to weep, and a time to laugh; a time to mourn, and a time to dance;

Verse 5: a time to throw away stones, and a time to gather stones together; a time to embrace, and a time to refrain from embracing;

Verse 6: a time to seek, and a time to lose; a time to keep, and a time to throw away;

Verse 7: a time to tear, and a time to sew; a time to keep silence, and a time to speak;

Verse 8: a time to love, and a time to hate; a time for war, and a time for peace.

CHAPTER I

WHAT MAKES A SOLDIER?

O ne crisp autumn day, I rushed home after work to our modest little house. Phyllis, my supportive wife and companion, met me at the front door and asked, "Did you pay your university class fees today?" "No," I answered. I never did pay my fees at the beginning of the semester because the lines were too long. Waiting in line was wasted time when you could be getting something done. I would usually wait and pay a week later; it was so much simpler. Her response: "Well, don't."

She handed me the official-looking document that began with "Greetings." The shock my wife must have felt when she opened the mail earlier that day to accept my selective service draft notice from a mail carrier. One can then fill in the remainder of the draft notice, indicating to report for induction to serve in the United States Army. I knew eventually that I would receive such a notice because I was reaching an age limit ensuring that I would probably end up in military service. Life as Phyllis and I knew it changed forever. Thoughts of war were seemingly so distant until that day.

The Korean War was a static, positional battle, a clash between the free world and Communism. Waging war from the southern tip of Korea at Pusan to the northern part and the

Yalu River, fierce, freezing Korean winters took the toll of many American GIs. Soldiers were unprepared mentally, physically, and militarily. It was a war fought by civilians-turned-soldiers, eating cold C-rations, World War II–vintage food sources, and wearing clothing not changed for several weeks.

"Though not officially a belligerent during the Korean War (1950–1953), the Soviet Union played a significant, covert role in the conflict. It provided material and medical services, as well as Soviet pilots and aircraft, most notably the Mikoyan-Gurevich (MiG-15) fighter jets, to aid the North Korean-Chinese forces against the United Nations Forces."[1] The Soviets backed the Korean War, and it did not get a lot of media attention.

"Combat was extremely fierce during the three years of war. Almost a million Chinese Communist troops joined the North Koreans five months after the war started. Americans fought in the Korean War to stop the military invasion of North Korean Communists. This was my first shock to Truman's decision to go to war. Before 1950 most people in the United States had never heard of Korea. Many soon became aware of this faraway peninsula. The United Nations Security Council voted to send troops to counter the invasion. Fifteen nations sent combat troops, and an additional five sent medical support. Ninety percent of the non-Korean United Nations troops were from the United States, and the overall command of the troops were by American generals" (***Unnamed Korean War Veteran***).

Many earlier battles, from 1950 to 1951, swept up and down the Korean Peninsula. "One such battle was the Battle of Bloody Ridge, a ground combat battle that took place during the Korean War from the 18th of August to the 5th of September

---

[1] http://en.wikipedia.org/wiki/Soviet_Union_in_the_Korean_War

in 1951. The battle began as an attempt by the United Nations (UN) forces to seize a ridge of hills which they believed were being used as observation posts to call in artillery fire on a UN supply road. Opposing armies jockeyed for position in the hills a few miles north of a line which ran from east to west."[2]

That forgotten war commenced for Phyllis and me when I, as a recently married young man, was hurrying home from a 3:00 to 11:00 p.m. shift job at Fulton Sylphon Company, a Knoxville, Tennessee, thermostat manufacturer, in September 1952. What makes a soldier? What happened to this newly married couple? Like so many others starting a career and a family, we received greetings to a painful struggle in a foreign land. Seeing civilians simply trained, clothed sparsely, and with limited weaponry of World War II vintage cross the Pacific Ocean to defend a land that most of the soldiers did not previously know existed. We defended ourselves from people we had never met, enduring hardship, fear, anxiety, and even death.

The Korean Peninsula was split in half after previous occupation by Japan until after the World War II victory. Japan was forced to surrender all of their colonies to the United States and Russia. Korea was split at the 38th Parallel, and a division resulted. Carved in the hearts and minds of the Korean people, the country was now identified as North Korea and South Korea. Each country took different paths as to social, economic, and political development. The different political ideologies boiled over when 75,000 North Korea People's Republic troops proceeded across the 38th Parallel on June 25, 1950. It has been more than a half-century since we, now veterans, were called to a three-year struggle that cost 55,000 casualties from

---

[2] en.wikipedia.or/wiki/Battle_of_Bloody_Ridge

the result of fighting the North Korean Communist Army. That line would be crossed and recrossed many times in an effort to tame Communist aggression.

Family

From a humble beginning, Harold Lloyd Maples was born on May 14, 1930. He grew up in Powell, Tennessee. His neighbors were of a generation filled with respect and honesty. Unlocked windows and doors were the rule of the day. A strong handshake confirmed a deal sealed with trust. There was no need to ask your neighbor for help. Your neighbor would come to your home willingly to work and build. There was a genuine bond between others. You could count on others to pitch in on the task at hand.

HAROLD,S HOME PLACE

Harold's home place

Generation after generation, the old barn is still standing strong. I was raised on a thirty-eight-acre farm to become the man I am today. My parents taught me without an uttering of words to appreciate the simple things of life and the wonders of nature. I saw the beauty in the misty rain and watched the fog lift on an unclear bottom of land. With the whisper of the wind, the weathered barn doors creaked and groaned as they were opened and closed. Nearby birds sang their songs. The fragrance of springtime flowers and trees filled the air. Plodding behind Dad and the mule-drawn plow, I watched as he tilled the freshly turned soil to prepare for planting. Row by row, each preserved seed was carefully and strategically placed beneath the earth; not too early and not too late. He took care to cover and protect the crops from the ever-changing weather. My dad said, "When the leaves on the trees turn inside out, a change in wind direction, that means it's gonna rain."

Dad and his team of mules

Instilled deep inside to this day, Dad and Mom were of the older generation. We grew up during the Depression. We had one horse, one cow, one pig, two mules, one wagon, and the always-necessary path out back to the outhouse. My dad, William Matthew Rhodes Maples, was a farmer. Myrtle Bell Roberts was a mother and a housewife. They worked from dusk to dawn raising their family and making their living farming the land. We got up with the chickens to begin our day. We went to bed along with the chickens at day's end. We carried our kerosene lamp from room to room, which provided minimum light.

William, in his early years, worked hard at the brickyard in Powell Station as a laborer, making brick. He always spoke fondly of his coworker Joe Latham: "A hard worker, he could toss brick faster than anyone I knew." My dad was a dedicated, competent employee, punctual, and a strong man who put in a full day's work for a few dollars; there was no such thing as an eight-hour workday. Unfortunately, he broke his leg on the job and as a result was let go. All the money he was able to save was lost during the Depression. The Depression brought on fifty-cent workdays, when work was available.

Myrtle worked just as hard tending to the animals, the garden, and so much more. Mom was religious, quiet, reserved, and dedicated to support her husband. She carefully collected eggs from the henhouse, washed our clothes with a hand washboard, and dried the clothes outside on a clothesline. Today this would be recognized as solar power. The only way of heating our home and cooking was to keep the wood fire going. A ton of coal was a luxury. Equally important was canning garden vegetables, preserving fruit, milking cows, filling the smokehouse with farm-raised meat, and drying out the walnuts—all to survive. My son, Lloyd, looked up to my dad as a pillar of strength. At the age of ten, he always took heart in what his Mamaw told him: "Greed, dishonesty, and laziness will be the end . . . if we let it. I won't see that day, but you will." This was a direct quote often used by my mom, along with: "Be good."

Mom and Dad

I found this tribute written by Larry Manar; it is a very descriptive writing portraying my mom.

Old-Fashioned Mom

You never told me

What I should be, or, what I should become.

You never said, "Be this," or "Be that,"

But just "Be good."

And somehow, in this magic way,

You always got across to me, what your expectations were.

And even if I did not deliver to you your wish,

I want you to know, that I always knew you expected good of me and . . . I always tried.

We survived by selling the harvested tobacco to the local market. The earnings were used at the local grocery store, J.E. Groners. We paid off previous credit for necessary staples, such as flour, meal, sugar. and kerosene. We were not going too many places or too far from home because we had no mode of transportation except a horse and wagon and walking. We were not that far removed from the true Appalachian area that is portrayed in Tennessee to this day by the local Museum of Appalachia, a pioneer mountain farm village. The museum is located in Norris, Tennessee, and the curator of the museum is Rice Irwin.

During this time, most of the people were dirt poor. Growing up through these difficult times was our way of life. We didn't know we were poor. There was always food on the table and a roof over our head. We made do with what we had. Nothing was ever wasted or thrown away. Even our scraps fed the pig. Possibly the only thing a pig won't eat are cucumbers, and neither do I. Natural resources provided the necessities of life in a rugged setting. There was a distinct pride of heritage in overcoming the Great Depression.

As a boy, my friend Calvin and I would go camping and fishing. We liked hunting for rabbits and squirrels and scavenging through the nearby woods. A few of our favorite pastimes were fishing in the ponds, spending time at the creeks, exploring, and enjoying nature. We learned to survive on our own by catching our meal, starting a fire, building a shelter, and learning which direction to go for home. Dad told me stories of his earlier years. One such story was of the hobos jumping off the train and beginning their trek toward the simple home of his mom, Matilda Maples. The hobos knew this Christian woman would never turn them away. She stretched her meager income of doing laundry for others to provide them with a hot meal. Sharing with the less fortunate was another rule of the day.

I was the youngest and had two older sisters, Leona "Lee" and Margaret Maples. Leona was my eldest sister. I looked up to her and confided in her. Margaret was a pillar of strength—quiet and reserved, like Mom. Both my sisters have a place this side of heaven, along with my parents.

Leona and Carolyn Maples

Margaret Maples

Only one school was available for my education. I graduated from Powell High School (PHS) on Spring Street with no strong desire to achieve a higher education. I had no aspiration to become famous. I was a poor student and disinterested in book learning. The great out of doors provided a perfect, fun learning laboratory. My high school teacher, Mr. Armstrong, was nothing short of a phenomenal teacher, going above and beyond. Other than family, he was one of the most influential people in my life. He believed in my potential to excel at whatever I set my mind to when I could not convince myself otherwise. Surprisingly, I was not too bad.

Mr. Armstrong encouraged me to try out for the basketball team, and I played center. He also convinced me to engage in the PHS junior and senior play. Juanita Mayes and I played the lead roles in the production of *The Valley of Ghosts*. Juanita, a pretty, petite blonde, was the heartthrob of many, myself included. J. T. Armstrong was the director of the play. I was scared almost out of my wits during rehearsals. It took a great deal of courage to set foot up on the stage in front of an eager audience. I was a person beyond shy and was very self-conscious. I never looked up to make eye contact with those around me, only seeing the ground. Thinking back, I still don't know how I learned the lines and performed in the play. It was suggested by some of the cast members that I could or should have gone to Hollywood because the walk would have done me good. After all, my parents named me after Harold Lloyd, a silent movie actor, so surely I had an advantage!

As a senior in high school, my first car was an ancient T-Model. It would be considered a collector's item today. My dad provided the twenty dollars to purchase the car from a University of Tennessee student.. At that time, twenty dollars was not easy to come by. Now I could go places, once I got it running. What a treat!

The first time I saw Phyllis Eleanor Keck was when I went to a high school square dance. My friend Barbara Popejoy may have been trying to do a little matchmaking, but it didn't pan out. She introduced Phyllis and me to each other. Later, Barbara asked Phyllis, "What do you think of Harold?" Phyllis replied, "He was with his girlfriend." I was with my sister, not a girlfriend. My social skills could have used some work, but things have a way of working out.

A pivotal point in my life was when I was invited to a Central High School (CHS) prom by my matchmaker, Barbara. I reflect back on the Powell High School square dance. The CHS prom was a double date. Phyllis was with Eddie and I was with Barbara. Ironically, my attention was more confined to the presence of Phyllis. Maybe there was a hint of jealousy.

On another day, it just so happened I had borrowed a one-and-a-half-ton truck to take a group of young folks on a hayride to the Smoky Mountains of Tennessee. I thought that I may be able to convince Phyllis to accept an invitation to come along. No time like the present to work on my social skills, I asked, and she accepted my invitation.

We quickly realized that we had a lot in common. Bouncing along at the end of the hayride, we headed back home. My social skills improving with practice, I convinced Phyllis to let me take her to meet my parents. We did just that. Phyllis was my motivation and incentive.

HAROLD AND BORROWED TRUCK...OUR DATING RIDE

What a ride

Phyllis was born on February 17, 1932. She was two years younger and lived in the community of Inskip, near Fountain City. So pretty and so incredibly smart, she learned to read before starting elementary school. She graduated from Central High School at the top of her class. Her favorite subjects were math, reading, and Latin. She was president of the Tri-Debs Club, which was composed of CHS girls. The other officers were Wanda Flannigan, vice president; Mary Lynn Thomas, treasurer; and Gail Moore, secretary. These women became special, lifelong friends. Phyllis and I went to the Tri-Debs Central High School's spring formal on a Friday evening at the Recreation Center. Dancing in the Dark was the theme. A black-themed background featured a silver silhouette figure dancing under silver stars. Jack Flower's orchestra played.

Never Been to School, but Is Wide Reader

And here's *Phyllis Eleanor Keck, daughter of Mr. and Mrs. Sherman Keck of Inskip, who will be 6 Feb. 17.*

Phyllis has never gone to school, yet has read two primers, a third reader twice, two second readers, a first reader and library and story books.

Phyllis

She can also spell in her spelling book and read the funnies.

Never been to school but is a wide reader

MISS PHYLLIS KECK, seated, has been elected president of the Tri-Deb Club, which is composed of Central High School girls. Other new officers are, left to right, Miss Wanda Flannigan, vice president; Miss Lynn Thomas, treasurer; and Miss Gail Moore, secretary.

Tri-Deb president Phyllis Keck

After graduating from Central High, Phyllis began her education at the Tennessee Business School. Her father could not pay for college, saying it was too expensive. No one, and I mean no one, could type faster than Phyllis on the manual typewriter. She began her career with the Tennessee Valley Authority in Knoxville, Tennessee, as an outstanding office secretary. Her long-lasting career was instrumental in both of us being able to retire early. I am beyond grateful for her help through my college efforts. We had dreams of starting a family soon and one day moving back to Powell Station to build on my home place. Life was good but challenging.

After graduating from Powell High School, my teacher, Mr. Armstrong, counseled me about going to college. I really had no desire, push, or the least bit of confidence that I could be successful as a university student. Mr. Armstrong insisted, and he took me to the University of Tennessee (UT) on the day of fall quarter registration. I found myself going through the registration process, obtaining a class schedule, and enrolling in school. What the heck, give it a shot. I made it through the fall quarter and quickly decided it may not be my thing. I packed my suitcase, and during winter quarter, I traveled to Pennsylvania to visit with my uncle Albert Roberts and family members. I gained youthful advice from family of a career pattern. It was time to think about what was next.

I felt pulled and pushed trying to convince myself that I had potential. Mr. Armstrong placed a small red book in my hand with the title *I Dare You.* This book helped me to try a new approach to the school of life. I received tons of support from so many caring persons who were helping to pay it forward.

Harold Maples senior high school picture

I came home after several weeks and re-enrolled in spring quarter at UT. I completed my courses with thoughts of the future running through my head. I convinced myself that higher education was not in my best interest. Mr. Armstrong said, "Perhaps moving and staying on a smaller campus may be a significant approach." With further counseling, he helped guide my direction and agreed to provide transportation for the move.

Financially, neither I nor my parents could begin to pay for such a luxury. The decision was to give it a try. With only $50.00 tuition in hand, I was dropped off at Tennessee Tech in Cookeville, Tennessee, as a transfer student from UT. I found myself alone in a new town and on a new campus. Without Mr. Armstrong's confidence in my ability, the following two years on Tennessee Tech's campus would not have been possible. I had the tuition for one quarter with no idea where the other resources would come from to pay for my education. I was allowed to bunk in a prefab dorm as a solution to lodging through the generosity of an administrator. I quickly trekked across campus and sought out the cafeteria manager, Mrs. Crawford, and was hired in food services, which provided some meal money. Working the gate at football games also added a few bucks. Hitchhiking home on weekends provided me with some food supplies and an occasional $10.00 gift from my oldest sister, Leona. There was no such thing as today's student loans.

I shared the prefab dorm mentioned with two roommates, W. C. "Sparky" Sparkman and William "Billy" Cruise. The room next door was vacant, so with a little construction effort, I was able to remove the back of the adjoining closet, hang a door, and make a study room and kitchen. An added hot plate encouraged trips to the grocery store and the ability to fix less-expensive meals. My favorite meals were hot dogs and spaghetti from the well-known brand, Chef Boyardee. This served well due to limited funds. Overall, this was a scary experience. This endeavor was a growth in progress and the fielding of much-needed personal confidence. After two years at Tennessee Tech, I transferred back to UT, mission accomplished. I re-enrolled and continued my course of study.

Hitchhiking home from Tennessee Tech was my mode of transportation to visit with Phyllis. We were together four wonderful years before I got up the courage to ask her father, Sherman Keck, for her hand in marriage. He granted his permission. Fortunately for me, she said yes.

"Miss Phyllis Eleanor Keck's engagement to Mr. Harold Lloyd Maples, Sr., son of Mr. and Mrs. W. M. Maples, Route 2, Powell, TN is announced today by her parents, Mr. and Mrs. Sherman Keck, 4708 Central Avenue Pike, Knoxville, TN. The wedding will take place July 12th, 1952" (***Knoxville News Sentinel, July 12, 1952***).

I now needed money for our honeymoon. As I left my 3:00 to 11:00 p.m. shift at Fulton Sylphon Company, there was an agent at the gate outside giving signature loans. I got a loan for $60.00 to pay for gas, room, and board for our honeymoon.

On a beautiful summer day, Phyllis and I had our ceremony in a small church, the Bookwalter United Presbyterian Church off Central Avenue Pike. It still exists today, now known as the Bookwalter United Methodist Church. Joyce, her older sister, and Joyce's husband, Jimmy, took part in the ceremony. We joined hands, united and committed to love and support one another for a lifetime of love. We did just that. She was the love of my life, my partner, and soulmate. After our wedding, Phyllis and I traveled to Myrtle Beach, South Carolina, for an amazing honeymoon.

A lifetime of love

Honeymoon

We moved into our very first home in July 1952, a white framed house with shingled siding and a front and back stoop. We were now in the quaint city of Maryville, Tennessee, located off Broadway, at 2413 Pennsylvania Avenue. We were about thirty miles from my home place. Our home met our needs. It was small, with two bedrooms, a living room, a kitchen, and one bath. This was the perfect little starter home for us. We would begin our family here with the birth of our son, Lloyd, and begin our journey to fulfill our dreams. Only there for a short period of time, we moved in October 1954 to West Maple Avenue in Fountain City. We had our second child, a girl, Karen Ann. Both of our children were born at Saint Mary's Hospital, in Knoxville, attended by Dr. Alton Absher. We were now a proud family of four.

First home

WE SOLD OUR HOME IN MARYVILLE TN IN OCT 54 AND MOVED TO
W. MAPLE AVE IN FOUNTAIN CITY

Second home

CHAPTER II

Two Soldiers on a Shared Journey

Harold kept a timeline of military dates and places he served. Throughout this book you will find timeline entries in all caps.

10 OCT 51 ORDERS FROM INDUCTION STATION (713 MARKET STREET, KNOXVILLE, TN) TO RECEPTION CENTER (FT. JACKSON, SC)

After receiving my draft notice, I (U.S.53–132–321) became just a number, the beginning of becoming an army soldier. The eventful day saw confused and lonely young men climb aboard a Greyhound bus bound for an unknown journey. Our first stop was basic training at Fort Jackson in Columbia, South Carolina. I was assigned to A-Battery 28th Field Artillery Battalion located on the beloved strip of ground known as Tank Hill, a water reservoir, thus the name.

Harold at induction, October '52 at Fort Jackson, SC

Boarding that same bus was a fellow recruit, Guy Metcalf (U.S.53–132–382), who would become a lifelong friend. We served together throughout the entire enlistment. The following is his own personal description for his entry into the army and our happenstance meeting:

> "I was nineteen years old when I was drafted into the United States Armed Forces. Washington State was hiring men for cutting and hauling timber in the dense forest. My oldest brother, Lattie and sister-in-law, Margie provided me an opportunity to work. Needless to say, the official greetings from Uncle Sam changed my plans drastically. I

traveled back to Greeneville, Tennessee, and onto the Induction Center in Knoxville, Tennessee. I arrived at the downtown Knoxville bus station for the ride to Fort Jackson, South Carolina, for sixteen weeks of basic training. Being the soldier that I was, I became squad leader" (*Guy Metcalf*).

Traveling the roads from the hills of Tennessee and the South Carolina mountains, two raw army recruits met for the first time. I met Guy while we were getting ready to catch the bus to Fort Jackson, South Carolina. I got my first look at becoming a leader when it was suggested that I march the men down to the bus station. I didn't know much about marching, but we made our way to load the bus.

Our journey began where our paths crossed. The journey started for a nineteen-year-old from East Tennessee. He was born Guy Shoun Metcalf, son of Henry Shoun Metcalf and Nola Matilda Thompson Metcalf. He graduated from the small town of Greeneville, Tennessee. Prior to his draft notice, he worked in the state of Washington. He traveled from the lumbering forests of Washington State, creating a springboard of life for us. Bussed together and anxiously awaiting deployment, Guy and I shared compassion, observation, and hope. We developed an unbreakable bond of friendship in basic military training. He was like the brother I never had. We shared the same geographical location, growing and changing together, a friend for life.

Guy Metcalf, a friend for life

Our orders were for sixteen weeks of basic military and heavy weapons training. When Guy and I talked about assignments, we were at Fort Jackson, South Carolina, where we got our orders for the Far East Command and Korea.

15 OCT 52 FORT JACKSON, SC—BASIC AND HEAVY WEAPONS TRAINING A—BATTERY— 28TH FIELD ARTILLERY BATTALION

21 NOV 52 QUALIFIED M-1 RIFLE AS A BASIC TRAINEE AT FT. JACKSON

Passes on weekends at Fort Jackson were not readily issued to trainees but were far and few between; and when they were, they were prized possessions. Checking around, I found out that by waiting until Saturday afternoon, I could go to the company charge of quarters. There were usually some passes that were not picked up. The brass was gone for the weekend, and some lonely clerk would be on duty. I would get a pass, and off I would go, home to see my wife. I never told anyone concerning my secret passes, although some buddies would question, "How did you get a pass?" I will have to admit the pass was restricted and did not cover the 285 miles needed to get home to Maryville, Tennessee, but as long as you were back for the Monday morning formation, no questions were asked. That was a lesson in military survival.

During the tenure of basic training, we were allowed weekend on-base visitors, and there were on-base guesthouses where family could stay. It was during one of these weekend visits that Phyllis had taken a bus to come visit. Our first car was an unreliable 1941 Ford. I had already driven the car to the base. We were always ready for our next road trip.

PHYLLIS IN OUR 1ST CAR
1941 FORD

Unreliable 1941 Ford

This weekend was our opportunity for something special; this was Christmas, December 1952. We were eager to be together on the base for our Christmas celebration. Phyllis arrived on Christmas Eve and waited for me at the guest-house to come in from the military field exercises for that day. I was able to obtain another weekend pass. Rather than stay on base, we made the decision to drive that night and have Christmas in our Maryville home.

Merry Christmas! Harold and Phyllis Maples

I was one tired soldier-to-be. After many days and nights in training and with little rest, we climbed into the old '41 Ford and started our Christmas journey home. It was late at night, and we were approximately sixty miles west of the army base when I became drowsy behind the wheel of the car. I saw the headlights of an oncoming car at an entrance road to my right. This road intersected the main road we were traveling on. My eyes were open, my hands gripped the steering wheel, and my mind was mentally dull and in a state of sleep. I assumed the oncoming car was on the main road and to my left. I vaguely thought I just needed to stay to the right. I turned down the intersecting road with plans to pass a stopped car to my right. The result was rolling off the roadway and striking a utility pole. Shocked and stunned from the impact, all I could think, "Is Phyllis okay?" Thankfully, she didn't sustain major injury.

Good Samaritans on this Christmas Eve night lived nearby. The Helms took us into their loving home. They took me to the hospital with a black-and-blue, swollen shoulder and then back to their home for the remainder of the night. Phyllis had a minor knee injury. She was in pain, but nothing was broken. A fellow soldier from Powell, Tennessee, L. C. Jenkins, was riding with us that night and sustained no injuries. He was able to catch a ride home that night by hitchhiking in a funeral home hearse. In need of repair, we left the car in Columbia, South Carolina, and caught a bus home.

I arrived back in time for Monday morning formation. Basic training with an injured right shoulder was no picnic, but I didn't want to be delayed to another training cycle. I requested to be allowed to carry my rifle on the left shoulder instead of on my right shoulder. Surprisingly, I was given permission. I don't think this was exactly standard training procedure, probably a first for military training.

06 FEB 53 PIPELINE TO FORT LEWIS, WASHINGTON

FEB 1953 SEVEN DAYS HOME DELAY EN ROUTE

At Fort Jackson, it was announced in a Company Street Formation that we would be shipping out. Fifty percent of our group would go to a European assignment and the remaining half to the Far East Command, which in simple words meant Europe or Korea. The fallacy in selection was that all African American trainees drew Europe, and all Caucasian trainees drew the Far East. This made me feel super special.

After completing training, I received a request to attend Officer Candidate School (OCS), which meant a longer year enlistment. I didn't hesitate to decline this as-signment. After completing basic training, Guy and I drew our seven days' delay en route to come home and be with our families. Then we took the troop train from Knoxville, Tennessee, to Fort Lewis in Washington to await shipping orders for pipelining to the Far East Region in Asia. The final destination was the unfamiliar land of Korea that was now engulfed in military conflict and fighting to repel communist aggression.

I remember well the day I pulled out of the Knoxville L & N Railroad Station, not knowing what the future held and if I would ever return home. After my wife dropped me off at the train station, I found myself thinking about the route Phyllis would be taking back home in the ole' '41. I believed that the service to your country was the right thing to do and at the same time wished that what was happening was just a bad dream, that I would wake up to a normal day—a warm, sunny fall day. A sudden jerk of the train brought me back to the realization that a new and unknown adventure was waiting and developing for my military buddies and me. I gained brief comfort in recognizing that many of my buddies reflected the same thoughts and concerns.

Thoughts of my wife, mom and dad, sisters, and in-laws became overwhelming. There were things I wished I had said to them. As I pressed my face against the train window, I got that last fleeting glimpse of my wife standing at the train station. Looking intently through misty eyes, I wondered how long it would be before we would be together once again; nine months, a year, maybe never this side of heaven. Was this my final boarding call? The train gained momentum, and I only felt the rocking of the train, the clicking of the wheels, and an empty feeling with unbelievable loneliness. Other soldiers near me were lightly joking among themselves to relieve tension. In their silence, we were probably experiencing the same feelings. And now—for the rest of the story.

The train arrived in Chicago with a switching of trains. We traveled cross-country north through the majestic Rocky Mountains, a major mountain range in western North America. Upon completion of our basic training, Guy and I were pipelined to the Far East Command, traveling to Fort Lewis, Washington. We arrived at Fort Lewis to wait on shipping orders. While in Fort Lewis, the military spent time organizing work details that had no particular purpose except to bug you and try to keep everyone busy: Fall out for detail, load the rocks on a truck, and take the rocks to another location. We rearranged the rocks and logs that had been rearranged by the detail before us. We then loaded back on the truck for our return to camp. It didn't take Guy and me long to realize that they were not checking as to who was in the details. Record keeping lacked precision.

The Road Less Traveled

"Metaphorically, the road less traveled means someone who is acting independently, freeing themselves from the conformity of others who choose to take the road often traveled."[3]

"Two roads diverged in a wood, and I—I took the one less traveled by, and that has made all the difference" (**Robert Frost**).

Guy and I made the decision to go rogue and take a road less traveled. He had a relative living in the lower part of Washington State. I asked him, "Why don't we go visit your brother?" Guy said, "Okay, we will do that." We decided to pay his brother, Lattie, his sister, Eva, and brother-in-law, David, a visit. We didn't have approved passes to go anywhere, but we went anyway. What's the worst thing they could do to us, send us to Korea?

So off we went, hitchhiking down to Deep River, Washington. We were picked up by a fellow driving by. We were riding with him in his car in the direction of his sister's home. As we were traveling, this car passed us, and I noticed two passengers inside. Out of my mouth, to Guy, came the words that those two people were his sister and brother-in-law. I had never met or seen his kin. Lo and behold, he looked out the car window and said, "It is them!" What a surprise! We quickly stopped, flagged them down,

---

[3] https://en.wikipedia.org/wiki/Wikipedia:Taking_the_road_less_traveled

and switched cars; continuing to the home of Guy's family. Guy couldn't figure out how I knew. We had a memorable visit with the Ball family.

17 MAR 53 2:00 P.M. TO VANCOUVER, CANADA SEA ISLAND AIRPORT AND FLIGHT TO TOKYO, JAPAN VIA COLD BAY, ALASKA SHEMYA ISLAND—(US AF BASE ALEUTIANS, TO PROV CO CAMP DRAKE, TOKYO, FLEW THE GREAT CIRCLE ROUTE

The three or four days in Deep River, Washington, didn't turn out so bad. They resulted in a welcomed commercial airline flying out of Vancouver, Canada, up over Cold Bay, Alaska, to the Aleutians, and into Tokyo. The original orders we missed drew us, along with other GIs, a flight rather than a ship ride across the Pacific Ocean to Tokyo, Japan, a first-class ride to Tokyo rather than a slow boat. It can't get much better than that. We missed the ship ride to Camp Drake, Tokyo, Japan. Was this luck or fate?

On March 17, 1953, our plane departed Vancouver via a small military base in Cold Bay, Alaska, for a fuel stop. Nothing but deep snow. All the facilities were underground except the runway! We were making our approach to the runway; only four or five miles long. It was announced from the pilot, "Buckle up. One set of runway lights is out, and the landing may be a little bumpy." Looking out the window, it was snowing like crazy. "A little bumpy" was an understatement. The DC-4 landed safely with only a single strip of runway lights. I suppose someone was giving us a good scare as payback for missing the ship. We had a safe landing on a short runway, a routine fuel stop, a bite to eat at the air force's expense, and then on our way to the Aleutian Islands. We arrived at Camp Drake in Tokyo, Japan, on March 19, 1953.

Harold at Camp Drake, Japan, March 19, 1953

Guy and I arrived many days prior to the ship that was carrying the rest of our troops. We were assigned duty to the supply line at Camp Drake to provide clothing and equipment to the soldiers arriving by the ship we should have been on. Buddies in line asked, "What are you two doing here?" We, of course, kidding, told the soldiers that we had permanent duty and were being stationed in Tokyo. "We are not going to have to go to Korea," we said. This was wishful thinking. They knew we were exaggerating the truth a bit.

30 MAR 53 ORDERS FOR ETA JIMA SPECIALIST SCHOOL (JAPAN) 04 APR 53 LEFT CAMP DRAKE— ETA JIMA, JAPAN

Duffle bags packed and work orders in our pockets, Guy and I left Camp Drake, and our journey continued to Eta Jima, Japan.

Duffle bag packed

05 APR 53 TO ETA JIMA, JAPAN—CBR SCHOOL

Fortunately, another happenstance occurred to Guy and me when we were both selected for a two-week specialized Chemical, Biological and Radiological (CBR) school in Eta Jima, Japan; thus delaying our inevitable shipment to Korea. Our two last names, Maples and Metcalf, being in alphabetical order on the roster, kept us together.

Guy Metcalf—Eta Jima

Guy Metcalf

Guy made this comment: "We were chosen to go to Eta Jima, Japan, to learn about atomic weapons—one such weapon that is impossible to reverse or undo."

We both wondered why we were chosen for this special training, with no rhyme or reason. Who knows? We arrived in Eta Jima, Japan, on April 5, 1953. Our schooling was held at a former Japanese naval academy, best described as the equivalent of the United States Naval Academy at Annapolis, Maryland; just the two of us again.

12 APR 53 VISIT TO HIROSHIMA, JAPAN

On April 12, 1953, we took a day trip on this Landing Craft Vehicle Personnel (LCVP) traveling ten miles across the bay to Hiroshima, Japan. We stood at ground zero where the atomic bomb was delivered in World War II and explored the destruction site. We monitored levels of radiation.

Eta Jima landing barge

Atomic bomb destruction

We were taught to be first responders in case of a chemical, biological, or radiological attack on Korean soil. The president at the time was Dwight D. Eisenhower. It is believed that President Eisenhower would have used the atomic bomb if the North Koreans had not come to some kind of agreement. The president made it clear that he would end the war in six months if it took dropping a nuclear weapon on Pyongyang.

President Dwight Eisenhower

Guy and I were grateful that a force of that magnitude was not necessary. There is an ethical debate to this day around the dropping of the atomic bomb. Yes, it might have brought an end to a destructive war, but would it have united the North and South Koreas, and at what cost? Nuclear considerations were studied throughout the war. The aftermath could have been so devastating. I can only guess as to how it would have impacted the two Koreas.

18 APR 53 GRADUATED CBR SCHOOL (TWO WEEKS TRAINING)

A defense training, CBR School trained us to be knowledgeable soldiers in case we got into an extreme situation in Korea. Though hard to comprehend, we understood. After completing the CBR School, we graduated on April 18, 1953, and received our certificate of proficiency from the Eta Jima Specialist School.

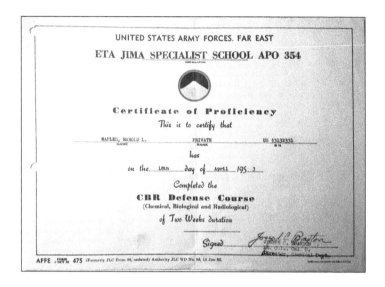

CBR certificate

18 APR 53 LEFT ETA JIMA, JAPAN

APR 19–22 APR 53 EASTER SUNDAY TRAIN TO SASEBO, JAPAN

We arrived in Sasebo, Japan, to catch a boat to Pusan, Korea. I was still stuck with Metcalf, or he was stuck with me. We were still sharing our routes together.

Still stuck with Metcalf

23 APR 53 5:00 P.M. BOAT FROM SASEBO TO PUSAN, KOREA

The overnight boat ride to Pusan was in the southernmost part of Korea. We realized this boat ride was not a cruise for fun and recreation, and there would probably be more days or weeks before we heard from home and family. I harbored the thought, *What happens next?*

Up until this point, I thought I was doing pretty well emotionally. The basic training infiltration courses at Fort Jackson were kind of fun; the new experiences fed the adventure-seeking side of my personality. Completion of training came with a thoughtful calm. This feeling of doing well faded when I received my orders. Basic training did not compare to waking up in Korea. Upcoming events were becoming more thought-provoking, resulting in serious nightmares.

CHAPTER III

RUDE AWAKENING

24 APR 53 8:30 A.M. ARRIVED PUSAN, KOREA—LEFT AT 3:30 P.M. VIA CROWDED NIGHT TRAIN RIDE TO 40TH DIV REPLACEMENT COMPANY—CHUNCHON

S ome call this Korean conflict the Forgotten War—but not to the ones who were there. I remember the crowded train ride and landscape en route to North Korea, the mission being to hold the line against Communism. We traveled the road that led to our station above the 38th Parallel in North Korea. The 40th Infantry, our unit, was a California Reserve Unit that was mobilized during the war.

Arriving in Pusan that day came with a noon meal of cold military rations from a can, maybe World War II C-rations, a far cry from home-cooked meals prepared by my mom and my wife, Phyllis. We were loaded on a truck and transported to a bleak, tented barbed-wire camp enclosure, toward the action.

The long train ride took us through this foreign land to my destination of an eventual assignment on the front line. Several months passed while we were in transit, and we didn't get a lot of mail. I didn't know what was going on at home. I was concerned, yes, beyond belief. On my way into the Pusan Military Compound, the realization of anxiety suddenly hit hard. Here I felt the reality of the situation, scared and uncertain. Other than boarding that bus to Fort Jackson basic training, this military compound experience was the most lonely feeling to date.

I was suddenly hit with the reality that, "Hey, man, I am a lonesome civilian-turned-soldier who is a long, long way from home. It is highly possible that I may not return to the ones I love most." Empty would not describe my feelings at this point in time. What's next in the series of unknown, upcoming events? At an all-time low in my life, my Creator and I had a good heart-to-heart conversation. What if something happens to me? What's going to happen to my family back home if I do not return to my loved ones I left behind? So many thoughts were racing through my mind about everything. I was reasoning with myself and trying to make sense of the senseless, looking for relief from apparent anxiety.

My infantry and heavy mortar training showed that my military skills and knowledge had advanced. I never thought that I was anything less than a soldier. The army has great ways to fill vacant slots and replacements. The reason for this type of training is to merely react to the situation at hand.

The ground in the area was almost barren, with the exception of these mounds. Having eaten my nourishing canned meal and with an opportunity to be alone, I walked to the far side of the compound to one of these hill-shaped mounds. I sat there a long time in the bright sunlight. Thousands of miles away from home, I realized this was not a game. I tried to convince myself that what will be, will be. I remember what Phyllis always said, "Things work out for the best." Realization hit hard. The decision was made; I may not make it back home.

Now, a soldier in God's hands, I told myself to make the most of it and quit worrying, to take one minute, one hour, one day at a time. As I climbed down from my perch, I was left alone to ponder my thoughts. I now had the opportunity to have a good talk with myself and get my head on straight. I regained some control and came to grips with the events. I learned later that the knoll I had crawled onto was, in fact, a Korean burial mound. How ironic? My innermost thought; this may be the place I face death. At that moment I realized that someday I may place my story in print.

Korean burial mound—Harold Maples

I am respectful of others' religious values and not always that religious myself. Was it fate or faith that got me through this war, coincidence or luck? I held on strong to my belief in God, though I had never been outspoken about that. What does God mean in my life? God is my pillar of strength. I count my many blessings each day and know that my wife lifted me up in her daily prayers. I always thought Phyllis had enough faith for both of us. Her strength and faith were immeasurable. She was my guardian angel; nothing else was important.

Phyllis endured anxiety, loneliness, childbirth, and sorrow alone. We held hands across the miles by writing daily letters to each other. I patiently waited for return mail or a telegram from home. In those days, any other type of contact was non-existent. The love we had for each other carried us through. I missed my wife, my love. I longed for her news from home; so far away, so out of touch. Lyrics from our love song: "Always: I'll be loving you always, with a love that's true always; When the things you've planned need a helpin' hand, I will understand always, always. Days may not be fair always, that's when I'll be there, always; Not for just an hour, not for just a day, not for just a year but always" (Irving Berlin).

Holding hands across the miles, Harold Maples

I remember the sights from the train to this day. Civilians, many refugees, military, and the 40th Infantry Division replacement company were on board. The lowest part of Korea was not too bad, after the original push down through Seoul and toward Pusan. The highest terrain was nothing but mountains and hills. Hostile action created orphans. I will never forget this Korean girl trudging along the road, carrying her brother or sister. Quite a load, almost the size of the carrier.

Korean girl carrying her little brother

The Pusan compound we were temporarily in was totally denuded except for the Korean burial mound. We were only there for part of a day, then on to our next life-changing stop. They put us on a crowded overnight train north to Chunchon, Korea. While boarding the train, we were told, "Don't be smoking, because a lighted cigarette might make you a good target." Whether truth or fiction, at least the suggestion got my attention. Packed like sardines, we chugged along up through the night and got into our replacement company.

We pulled into the train station. We were only at the compound a couple of days. On a few nights of guard duty, reality hit hard again as I watched the distant artillery flashes at the front. We were considered the rear area. I thought we had it made, being in the rear compared to those men defending the front.

Seeing Korean men rounded up from the village to form troops forever sticks in my memory. It was so different from the United States draft experience. Republic of Korea (ROK) soldiers encircled the young men to draft them and proceeded to march them off for battle. We recovered about six or seven of the ROK soldiers who had been killed by mortar rounds. They cremated them onsite.

ROK soldiers training with wooden guns

25 APR 53 5:30 P.M. ARRIVED CHUNCHON 40TH DIVISION REPLACEMENT COMPANY

We spent a few days at Chunchon as a temporary assignment to the compound duty, awaiting orders to move further north. I thought, hey, we are going up front anyway. Why don't we go on a little sooner? We arranged a situation. If we shot a round back in the rear area, they had to report it. So, we accidentally let a few go off while working guard duty. The next thing we knew we were leaving Chunchon.

04 MAY 53 1812 MOS—SUIN-NI, KOREA— REFRESHER COMBAT SCHOOL—ARRIVED 4:30 P.M. (FOUR MILES NORTH OF 38 DEGREES PARALLEL)

Guy and I remember the location and the month we arrived in Suin-ni, Korea: the spring of 1953, on May 4. We saw our destination draw nearer to the front lines in what was known geographically as the Punch Bowl. We saw intense nighttime flashes of artillery in the distance, lighting up the sky.

Our assignment was to move forward to Suin-ni for five to six days of refresher combat training. We were issued rifles and ammo for that time period. We even got a picture of the two of us still traveling together. After the few days of refresher training, it surprised us that our weapons and ammo were taken up before we were sent on our merry way. This was a little bit confusing being sent forward without weapons. We were told reissuing would occur when we got to our company. It seems that there was a method of accountability of equipment. I didn't realize this was a concern; was it politically motivated?

Refresher combat school

11 MAY 53 LEFT SUIN-NI—TO SERVICE COMPANY—PUNCH BOWL (BASIN) KNOWN AS WHITE REAR—GRAVES REGISTRATION—SERVICE COMPANY, 224TH INFANTRY REGIMENT, 40TH DIVISION—QUARTERS WERE A BUNKER AND BUNKER BATHS—ROUTE TO PUNCH BOWL VIA PUK-HAN RIVER; YAGGU PASS; STEEL POT LINE

After they took up our ammunition, we were loaded on trucks. Leaving Suin-ni, we convoyed via Yaggu Pass on our way to the Punch Bowl. This was a landmark above the dividing line that placed us closer to the front line in North Korea. We passed a sign that read Steel Pot Line; time to ponder the reason for headgear. As we approached the Yaggu Pass, we crossed the Puk Han River and traversed narrow, temporary roads in a mountainous area. In basic training, we had been trained in heavy weapons, and the assumption was that we would go on line with a company in that capacity. We arrived at the base of the Punch Bowl on May 11, 1953. This was our first glimpse of hostile-action territory.

Yaggu Pass—Puk Han River

Looking down into the Punch Bowl, I saw that this part of Yaggu Pass had been an area of heavy conflict. A great deal of fighting and loss of life took place in this northern natural, rimmed geological bowl encircled with steep, jagged mountains. This was a large, circular valley with limited road access at the edge of the western front. Road access made movement of equipment and personnel particularly challenging. As a result of heavy mortar shelling, the view of what once was a spectacular vista was left barren, with only a few shattered trees. This is a photo looking down into the bowl from the rim. Early engagements during the war saw only mountainous footpaths and narrow trails for military vehicles. Today the Punch Bowl is some of the largest and richest farming land in South Korea.

View looking down into the Punch Bowl

We were reassigned to Service Company, 224th Infantry Regiment, 40th Infantry Division, thus supporting the fighting front. We were routed to our living quarters, which were bunkers constructed from logs and sandbags. We lived in a one-room sandbag bunker with four guys and a host of rats. Rats had their midnight parties and shared our quarters, scampering and urinating on some soldiers. The rodents contaminated our food and water with their urine and feces. We learned later that the demise of some soldiers was from hemorrhagic fever carried by rats.

The first question I was asked as I was going through the processing line, "Can you type? You might be reassigned to service company if you can type." I thought this was a strange question. I suppose they had noted that I had some college studies. I asked, "What would I be doing?" The answer: "You would remain here in Graves Section and process personal effects." My thought was that this positioning was better than being closer to the front and heavy weaponry.

Needless to say, I fibbed and said I could type. I wrote home to Phyllis and asked her for a quick typing lesson. She wrote back to let me know the home keys on a typewriter, and I did a little practicing. It turned out that advanced typing skills were not an important requirement. The portable, vintage, manual typewriter was merely used for typing routing tags; therefore, two-finger typing was sufficient to get the job done. A little white lie was eventually forgiven. Another section member did the occasional typing; I didn't have to fulfill this assignment.

To further my confusion, I assumed personal effects were items that you would find on one's person. I had no idea that they were talking about persons who were killed in action (KIA) and required locating, transporting, and evacuating bodies. The tags I typed were body tags. The fib ended up becoming a new assignment of unknown entailment. The shocking part was that I had never experienced a funeral before and had no idea what was in store. I trekked across the way to the bunker that housed five other section members.

I was greeted by Dennis Hultgren who asked, "Can you drive that truck out there?" I said yes, since I had practice in stretching the truth. This is how I ended up in Graves Registration. Though a difficult and dutiful assignment, I may have avoided heavy weapon action on the front, although the route I would take was to the front to reach the KIAs.

Graves Section bunker—Harold Maples

I turned and looked back to see my friend Guy in a distant line of troops. I assumed he would be positioned online for heavy weapons. I said to myself that we would be parting. I turned around to the assigning personnel and said, Hey, I got a buddy back there. Do you think we can keep him here with us? They said, "Probably." My buddy Guy was also assigned to service company, but in ration breakdown. Both assignments were equally dangerous and hazardous. We sat back from the front, receiving incoming rounds of artillery. Guy traveled up and down the dangerous roads via the front line, and he and I continued close contact, as had been the situation from our original enlistment. Guy told his side of the story:

"There were five men in my section along with Koreans to help. We were to obtain and ferry food rations and sustainments from the Quartermaster Corps Area to the front-line troops. We would take five 2 1/2-ton trucks to haul these rations. I loaded 600 to 800 packages of C-rations on each truck. The drop-off point was mess halls or kitchens. We didn't have open fire at drop-off. If we passed the artillery line, we were out of order.

"On a below-freezing day in the Punch Bowl, I went back to three military heavy weapons batteries that shot, boom, boom, boom, boom, then all together. This was up on the rim of the Punch Bowl. We had to set up a perimeter defense because we were in a bad spot. We were far more fortunate than most GIs.

"The food probably came from Inchon. We weren't all that far from Seoul. I went back to Seoul once and got to sleep in a bunk bed with sheets and pillowcases.

"No tanks were in our positions. We lost a few trucks when they wouldn't go into gear while going up a steep hill at the end of the Punch Bowl, never seeing the driver again. It was pitch-black, and we couldn't see ahead of us. We weren't supposed to have a light of any kind. I was lucky not to be hit by enemy fire as many times as I crossed the line. I was so cold my breath made icicles."

Ration breakdown bunker—Guy Metcalf

Guy Metcalf—Korea

Guy Metcalf and Harold Maples—TI&E

My first mail call came with all of the month's mail and packages that had been en route—letters, crumbled homemade oatmeal cookies, and all the news. A kind of peace at last! I hardly noticed the flashing of mortar rounds and the sound of gunfire all around me. After all, Phyllis and I were expecting our first child. Months passed with extreme conditions, with monsoon rains that were colder than cold. The weather did not stop our daily duty. As I journeyed up toward the front line to retrieve soldiers killed in battle, I found out the true meaning of Graves Registration. War is hell.

A belated telegram arrived with the news: "*It's a boy!* Both doing fine. 7 pound 6 Ounce Boy, September 22nd, Wife Baby Doing Fine Phyllis." Phyllis showed my firstborn a picture of his dad from her hospital bed. Our son—I couldn't have been more proud. It would be a while before I would hold him in my arms. I was experiencing a feeling of being home and yet so far away. I always carried this picture of my wife and son.

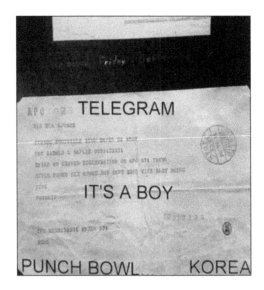

Telegram—it's a boy

Firstborn, my son

CHAPTER IV

GRAVES REGISTRATION (DIGGER'S REST)

S ergeant Dennis "Clem" Hultgren had completed his army duty and was rotating home. In the photograph below, Dennis Hultgren stands proudly to the right of Harold Maples. The unbreakable bond between soldiers is strong. Private Maples replaced Sergeant Hultgren in Graves Registration (Digger's Rest). Dennis, from an ancestral farm in Akron, Iowa, and Harold from the hills of Powell, Tennessee, crossed paths if only for a short time. Prior to his journey home, Dennis and I went on an authorized tour of the rim of the Punch Bowl for orientation to acquaint me with the area I would be patrolling. Our mission was to get oriented with the road to the frontline so that we could retrieve those killed in action (KIA).

> "Harold and I remain friends to this day, staying in contact with each other and visiting each other's homes" (*Dennis Hultgren*).

Friend Harold Maples from Tennessee and Dennis at the "Punch Bowl".
We have remained friends up to the present time.

Harold Maples (L) replacing Dennis Hultgren (R)

Graves Registration:

- **Lt. Wilfred E. Smith—Danville, Illinois**

- **Dennis Hultgren—Akron, Iowa**

- **Howard Hinkle—West Virginia**

- **Keith Daily—Chicago, Illinois**

- **Darryl Sweeny—Kentucky**

- **Gene Schoch—Pennsylvania**

- **Harold Maples—Powell, Tennessee**

Graves Registration, Dennis Hultgren

Dennis Hultgren described his job:

> "We had to drive up to the area just behind the front lines almost every night to pick up the dead. Sometimes there would be one killed, and sometimes we had seven or eight KIAs. This was in North Korea, and it was a very dangerous duty for the young men who were on patrol.

Frontline

"I have been asked if I ever have trauma because of my experiences in Korea. This is especially true during my work with the KIA soldiers who were taken directly from the battlefield. I do know that my life has been affected. It concerns the difference of the young dying compared to the old dying. Let me explain. Inevitably death comes to everyone. Anyone who has lived a full life, raising a family, enjoying grandchildren and perhaps even great-grandchildren has certainly had fulfillment and a successful completion of life on this good earth. No disrespect intended, I do not mourn for the death of the old in the same way that I mourn for the death of the young. This has been the main result of any trauma as a result of my service in Korea.

"I am thankful to the Lord that I did return without mental or physical injury. A relative told me when I got back that it was predestined that I would return all right. This is a very difficult theological question for me. I have always believed that we are responsible for our own actions. Decisions we make ourselves have a great effect on the lives we live. My decision to go to leadership school changed the timing for my arrival in Korea. My decision to raise my hand and indicate to assigning personnel that I knew how to type no doubt had a great effect on my army service. Those two decisions were my own. Perhaps the Lord guided me to make them; I don't know. I think that it is egotistical to believe that a person is so important that the Lord would give special importance to him."

Graves Registration War Department Field Manual

"I never really worried about what could happen to me in Korea. You have no control of it anyway. You do worry that if the worst should happen, how this would impact your mother and family. I have read when a young soldier dies in war, his last words and thoughts are of his mother.

"I will never regret my service to my country. I will remember it all to the end of my life. My story helps me remember. I know that I will be the most enthusiastic reader of it. I will read it all again, and again, and yet again.

"Below is a photo of two of our Graves Registration men working on servicing our trucks. The trucks were used for all our responsibilities for those killed in Korea. The one on the left is Harold Maples" (Dennis Hultgren).

Harold Maples (L) and unknown soldier (R)

The preceding extended quote from Dennis was a testimony of the camaraderie of soldiers and a dutiful performance of like individuals. He shared his story and photo. He dedicated this to his grandchildren. You can find the article in its entirety in the *Graybeards* Magazine, entitled "The Reminisce."

Home away from home, Digger's Rest, is a specialty that is instilled in my mind. On our arrival at the Punch Bowl, I was assigned to my suite shared by four other soldiers in Graves Registration. Bunkers were positioned in the Punch Bowl. The enemy had been driven back north of the 38th Parallel. The fighting had evolved into a static defensive combat of bunker, trench, and small patrol units. The hills were nearly bare, and foliage was nonexistent from heavy shelling up and down the hills. Fortunately, the casualties at this stage of the war were considerably fewer in number but no less important to the cause.

The earlier battles saw many GIs lose their lives, or they were taken prisoner. KIAs were interred in temporary grave sites. Mounds of bodies were processed on South Korean soil and eventually returned home. Earlier battles did not allow immediate evacuation. Providing the first leg of the homeward journey of military personnel killed in action was an honor. Many are still unaccounted for, but efforts continue to locate those missing in action. The conflict of this war has left a lasting effect that is still felt today.

Digger's Rest—Harold Maples

Digger's Rest—Howard Hinkle

Graves Registration had the duty of being the delay squad, aptly described as sacrificial lambs, and not likely to survive. Not an attack unit, we were positioned in the rear to delay the enemy until the company could withdraw, thus maintaining a defensive position. Our bunkers were in range of enemy fire as we evacuated both United States and enemy soldiers.

SCHOCH - HINKLE - DAILY - SWEENEY

Gene Schoch, Howard Hinkle, Keith Daily, and Darryl Sweeney

The first bodies and personal effects that I picked up were the enemy's. I eventually advanced into picking up fellow United States soldiers. We were given a code name, and they would call us on an old field phone when they had somebody we needed to recover.

This was extremely difficult, but somehow I was able to complete the job. Never easy, I recovered and collected their belongings. If a KIA, any personal items on them went with the body, no matter what the situation. We returned them to the company for processing. Thank God, I didn't process any of my known buddies. I knowingly processed one acquaintance who I recovered. Death comes to us all, with no control over when or how. Casualties were placed in body bags and brought back to the company morgue tent for identification. Here we were able to process them more readily instead of having to inter them in mass graves. The soldiers were ready for their final journey home.

Bruce Johnson, David Evans, George Campbell, Fred Ellick, Ed McMullen, Harold Maples

Later orders moved us from the Punch Bowl up to the rim of the bowl, just a location. We were there for a period of time. We then moved into Kumwah Valley and Chorwan Valley. On the rim of the bowl, there was not much of a road. Trying to go up the mountain at night was a hazardous situation. One of the dual wheels would be hanging off, over the side of the cliff. One dark, cold night, I went up this narrow road. Naturally you could not have any light, nothing to draw the enemy's attention to your location. The truck driver followed me up there as I walked. I carried a little cat-eye flashlight on my hip just in case of an emergency. I have to give the military credit where credit is due. They were going to respectfully take care of those KIAs, no matter what—no man left behind.

There were personal items that the soldiers had on them that stood out. I found a lost camera. I always think about one GI. He got hit so hard by artillery that the coins in his pocket were indented, more than likely a direct hit. This was the only decision I made not to send a personal item back with the soldier. I may have been wrong, but I just couldn't visualize sending those coins. There weren't a whole lot of remains left.

Howard Hinkle (L) and Harold Maples (R)

KIA on Forward Slope

An unidentified body was on the forward slope of a mountainous valley, and we were called to check this out and identify him. Being on the forward slope placed the situation in open view of the enemy firepower. At that time, the condition was foggy and provided sufficient cover to check the reported KIA. A closer look noted a foot protruding from the group was wearing Chinese-issue footwear and was not a GI. The fog suddenly lifted, and small arms fire was incoming. We made a hasty return to a safer position.

A point of interest is that we occasionally would recover enemy KIAs and process those to the rear area. Part of the process, not sure why, was to strip, wrap in GI blankets and load on a truck. In removing clothing and personal effects, the items they had were meager, and my attention would be called to the winter- or summer-issue footwear. The winters were bitter cold. In removing the footwear, I noticed the feet had been wrapped with knotted pieces of cloth in an effort to keep warm. The eyelets in the footwear would fall out, indicating that the footwear had not been removed since original issue. It was common to find the enemy wearing GI clothing and carrying other personal items. An example of a personal item, United States military payment certificate which was paper money issued for temporary use.

The Allied nations stood their ground; a chilly front for everyone. The war separated thousands of Korean families and created the most heavily fortified border in existence. This was a splintered nation with the lingering threat of dismantling the armistice because of the United States' presence on the peninsula and so-called war moves. The American and United Nations flags flew proudly in the Company of Wonju, Korea.

The American and United Nations flags

Another situation from this standpoint was our section's sergeant. We covered for him. Mentally the trauma of the assignment got to him! To be honest, it got to us all of us in one way or another. Some of us just hid it better. Everybody experiences trauma; life and death merge in an instant. Post-traumatic stress—what was that? It was not in our vocabulary.

Smoke Valley, Korea, East Central location, in July 1953 was covered with smoke from dozens of generators. The smoke covered the road to obscure enemy observation by communist artillery as vehicles and troops moved along the open road. Smoke Valley was so named because the enemy occupied the hills with embedded tunnels. Overlooking and controlling the higher ground, the enemy could see our troops and vehicles approaching on a small half-mile stretch of road. We were heading directly into enemy fire, zeroed in by their weapons.

Smoke Valley Road

Smoke Valley chapel

Smoke was generated in that stretch of road to block the enemy's sight as we moved up and down the road toward the front lines. This smoke surrounded us as we moved through the area without drawing mortar fire. Keeping an effective smoke screen allowed vehicles to travel through with less risk. We received a call. Our assignment was to pick up soldiers; we were not sure how many.

Smoke Valley collage

Etched forever in my mind, on my way up to the front lines to pick up KIAs, I saw a small military chapel to the side of the road. On this smoke-filled Sunday morning, I decided to briefly stop at the military chapel and go inside for the Sunday service in Kumwah Valley.

Military chapel

I was only there for a short time, and while I was inside the church, the smoke lifted by a brisk wind on the road a few miles ahead. Our enemy pounded this stretch of the road with intense artillery and mortar fire. I know my guardian angel was looking down on me that day. The stop in the chapel was a blessing in disguise. This chapel stop probably saved my life.

Passing thought: hygiene was not a priority, as you can imagine. We had no baths for three months. We used our helmets for wash pans to clean up, occasionally heating the water on a fuel stove. My day is never complete now without a shower.

Gene Schoch, Darrel Sweeney, Harold Maples—Punch Bowl

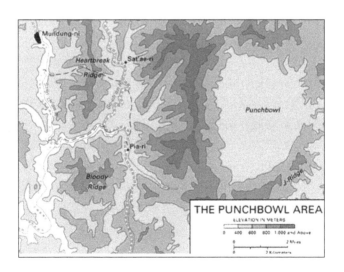

Punch Bowl map

17 JUN 53 RANK PROMOTION (PFC) 40TH DIVISION—224TH INFANTRY— SERVICE COMPANY

02 JULY 53 AWARDED COMBAT INFANTRY BADGE (CIB)

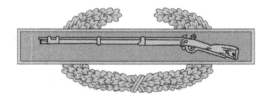

Combat Infantry Badge

07 JULY 53 UNIT MOVED TO RIM OF PUNCH BOWL—A TIME OF KOREAN MUD

JULY 53 WHILE LOCATED ON RIM OF PUNCH BOWL, SIGMUND RHEE RELEASED ALL POWS ON KOJO—DO; QUITE A STIR

At the time of the armistice, South Korean president Syngman Rhee was known for his political position to try to stop the negotiations. In July 1953 President Rhee did not see any advantage to the peace talks that would leave a portion of Korea in communist hands. He surprised the negotiators on both sides when he tried to stop the negotiations. He released about 25,000 North Korean prisoners of war (POWs). President Rhee said, "The prisoners showed a desire to remain in South Korea after the war." This was also quite a shock to the soldiers along the 38th Parallel front lines as to what could be unexpected from this release. We were positioned on the landmark, the rim of the Punch Bowl. As previously mentioned, our squad assignment on the delay squad came with the responsibility to hold action in case of enemy breakthrough from the frontline. This gave us great concern, not knowing if the released POWs would become rearmed and be to our rear. Only sparse ammo was available in our ammo dump at that time. We wanted this war to be over so we could return home to our families.

JULY 53 LEFT PUNCH BOWL—UNIT MOVED TO SANDBAG CASTLE—QUARTERS WERE TENTS

I recall the ravages of war, noting death on the field of battle and seeing soldiers make the supreme sacrifice for the sake of freedom. How quickly some forget the sacrifices made.

Sandbag Castle—July 1953—Harold Maples

CHAPTER V
NO-MAN'S LAND

W e had been hearing rumors for several weeks that this police action was almost over and that a ceasefire would be announced. Rumors, as we learned, do not stop fighting. Our unit had just moved from the rim of the Punch Bowl and positioned itself on the line along with the two other 40th Regiments, the 160th and the 223rd. On July 17, 1953, the 224th Regiment moved near Satae-ri in the Sandbag Castle Sector and was now located north of the 38th Parallel.

Harold Maples and soldier's boot

The threat of nuclear action probably helped move the armistice forward, not a peace treaty. The negotiation of President Eisenhower and military leaders ended the fighting, guns falling silent after three years of fighting, thus creating the new boundary at the 38th Parallel, a buffer zone of two and a half miles between North and South Korea, thus ceasing a war that's not dedicated to victory, characterized by President Truman as a "police action."

Stalemate

Rhee's action resulted in an airborne regimental combat team that had returned to Japan, ordered back to Korea. The Chinese front had renewed their efforts for one final battlefield effort against South Korea. Finally, on Monday, July 27, 1953, both sides signed the settlement and the ceasefire occurred at 10:00 p.m. on that day.

What were you doing the day the truce was signed?

My memory of the last hostile casualty of our 224th Regiment occurred just short of the ceasefire agreement. I do not have the soldier's name and would be reluctant to research military records due to the possibility of error. Not having the person's name does not replace my vivid memory of the situation of this young soldier. It is beyond my comprehension to explain the reason for what happened. Once again I can only surmise. What if they hadn't run out of some equipment?

I will always remember the young casualty, a new replacement for one of the line companies. This new arrival was checking in at the supply section for his equipment before moving on up to the front. Equipment, as most GIs knew, was always sadly lacking. I was unaware of when flak jackets were made available to troops as a regular item to help protect soldiers from artillery fire.

Equipment lacking

The unfortunate lack of availability of a flak jacket resulted in an untimely—and possibly unnecessary—death. Within a few hours of the new soldier's arrival, our Graves Registration received a call on the field phone concerning a KIA. When I arrived at the site, I was dismayed to find that the soldier was the one I had seen earlier at supply. Needless to say, he was minus the flak jacket! His wound was caused by a small but lethal mortar shell fragment that had penetrated his chest. No doubt the jacket would have saved his life.

My thoughts at that time, and now, were that the soldier's parents and loved ones were hearing the ceasefire news and were probably thinking that their loved one had escaped harm's way and would come home safely. Many years later, memories of this young soldier linger in my mind, along with others of a similar nature. The most significant, however, is how the role of this young casualty played out. I can only wonder about one of the worst scenes in my memory: a missing piece of equipment. The missing flak jacket could have saved this young soldier's life. I wish I knew more about his earlier life, his family and friends, his ambitions never realized.

The Korean War shaped the lives of many. We would be remiss if we didn't honor those children who were victims of misplaced lives—and missing flak jackets. It was such a heavy price to pay. I later wrote an updated story entitled "The Missing Flak Jacket" and submitted it to the Korea War Veterans Association *Graybeards* Magazine. My article generated responses from both fellow soldiers and soldiers' families.

A Buddy Remembers

"I believe I have some important information for you regarding the unnamed GI in your Graybeards article, 'The Missing Flak Jacket'" (**Nick Spartichino**).

Sergeant Nick Spartichino was buddied up with PFC Robert "Bob" Walker Bernier, of Dorchester, Massachusetts, for two brief days. Both soldiers served in the 224th Regiment of the 40th Division, Item Company. Their unit was located in Kumwha Valley at Sandbag Castle Sector, and they were both members of the second squad under squad leader Sergeant Sproul. Robert was assigned to the same bunker as Nick. The bunker was on an extremely steep slope. This war-torn scenario was playing out just prior to the ceasefire, and at this particular time, except for a few incoming mortar rounds, it was an eerie calm.

From his bunker, Nick's military operational assignment was to rig napalm explosives that were strategically placed in different line positions to deter enemy approach. These explosives consisted of five-gallon cans of napalm. Each can was numbered with battery leads to each of the numbered cans for detonation. Nick, on this particular night, had the task of waiting and watching for any enemy movement while seated on a steel rim with a piece of cardboard for an uncomfortable cushion.

Nick met Robert the next morning after his overnight napalm duty. They sat down to breakfast and had chow together. After breakfast they went down to a nearby stream at the crest of the hill for some personal hygiene and shared conversation together. Nick wrote:

"A short time later, Sergeant Sproul chose Bob for a detail to carve out some steps on the steep bunker incline. The steps should make access a little bit easier when the ceasefire took place. The withdrawal and supply route would be less difficult to navigate up and down the one-and-a-half-mile pullback zone. The steps did not get completed. Bob was hit with a small fragment of a mortar round. I was informed by Sergeant Sproul that Bob didn't make it.

"We had to sign a paper that day stating we would not fire unless we were fired at. Later that day I was skylined and shot at by an automatic weapon. Quite a sobering thought if the shots had been a little lower.

"Night came, and it sounded like a bunch of Fourth of Julys all together. At 10:00 a.m., just like that, it stopped. You could hear a pin drop. A few minutes later, something very heavy was fired from our side, three rounds. The next day I was picked to go to all the bunkers with a burlap sandbag and remove all the grenades and bring them to the supply tent. I went to a number of bunkers and was on the way to other bunkers when I smelled powder burning. My first thought was that the grenades were ready to go off. It would not make any difference if I threw the bag away because there was no safe place to get rid of it. I rounded a bend, and there was a medic who had taken a grenade apart and was burning the powder. Whew!

"The following day we were loaded onto trucks and we left Sandbag Castle. On the way, an elderly Korean man, a *papasan*, pointed to the sun. The reason this had any meaning was all insignia was removed from all the trucks. How did he know it was the 40th Division? Our patch was the sun with a blue background. We got to our destination and started the long climb up the mountain. At first, the climb wasn't bad, but the higher we went, the worse it got. All the work soldiers did to carve steps did not help. When we started up the mountain, it seemed that for every three steps you took, you slid back two steps.

"We reached the top and pitched our pup tents. All our supplies had to be carried up from the valley. The one time I remember most was the cardboard case of six number ten cans of string beans. I started out with them on my right shoulder for about 200 yards, then to the left shoulder. I kept changing shoulders, and the distance grew shorter and shorter. When I got about twenty feet away, I did not know if I'd make it. From there I went to my tent and flopped down. Hours later when I woke, I found out I slept on a can of C-rations and never knew it at the time. I remember standing on a ridge and looking down at a flying helicopter and saying, 'Today I am a man.' It was my twenty-first birthday.

"We stayed on the mountain about three weeks. I was told to go to the valley for instructions on the Browning automatic rifle. We were questioned on what we knew. In my case, it wasn't much. We were asked to name each part the instructor showed us. I could not name a single piece. We were given manuals to study. The next night, I was prepared; I named every piece the instructor held up. The next thing I knew I was a Browning Automatic Rifleman (BAR). We then had instructions on taking it apart and putting it back together. I have to say I got pretty good at it. Later it came in very handy" (*Nick Spartichino*).

After only two days serving together, PFC Bernier lost his life prior to the ceasefire. The date of loss was July 26, 1953. On this same day, Nick received enemy fire from an automatic weapon, thankfully all misses. Nick could have easily been the last KIA. Exposed to enemy fire, the unnamed soldier with his missing flak jacket now has a name, PFC Robert Bernier, the last hostile casualty of the Korean War.

"This photo is of our inspection and parade grounds. It is faded, and the text is almost unreadable. It was taken in Kumwha Valley and developed in Japan when I was on R&R. The sign contains the 40th Infantry Division 224th Crest as well as the Combat Infantry Badge.

"After the inspection and in Bob's memory, the company dedicated the field as the Robert W. Bernier Field. I don't remember if it was the captain of Item Company or the battalion commander who dedicated the field. I cannot recall who built the memorial sign. It's been a long time ago" (***Nick Spartichino***).

Bernier Field, named in honor of PFC Robert W. Bernier, killed in action July 26, 1953, Sandbag Castle

"The Missing Flak Jacket" story in *Graybeards* magazine had caught the eye of other fellow soldiers. This resulted in

a welcome exchange of phone conversations, subsequent letters, and memories—their own recollection of their service
in the military. An incredible exchange followed regarding
the happenings around the ceasefire between proud veterans
brought together long after the war—once strangers, now
friends. It is amazing that over the miles and years there are
still meaningful contacts made between and among veterans.

The Korean War made a lasting impression on many
mentioned heroes in this publication. Heroes such as Robert
Bernier, Leo Bromleny, Dennis Hultgren, Guy Metcalf, and
Nick Spartichino are only a few of the servicemen who
fought for their country; they were not just numbers.

**27 JULY 53 CEASE FIRE—TRUCE—ALL THREE
REGIMENTS (223RD, 224TH AND 160TH)
WERE ON LINE—AT THE TIME OF THE CEASE
FIRE, THE 224TH INFANTRY MAIN BATTLE
STATIONS WERE AT SATAE-RI (SANDBAG CASTLE
SECTOR)—THE CEASE FIRE WAS AT 2200 HOURS
(10:00 A.M. KOREAN TIME), AND AS REQUIRED
BY THE TERMS OF THE CEASE FIRE AGREEMENT,
ALL PERSONNEL AND MATERIALS WERE TO
BE EVACUATED TO THE SOUTH, CREATING
A "NO-MAN'S LAND" WITHIN SEVENTY-TWO
HOURS OF THE CEASE FIRE. TOTAL
EVACUATION WAS COMPLETED AT 1800 HOURS
(6:00 P.M.) ON 30 JULY 1953.**

A ceasefire forthcoming and now the long-awaited event
of the summer of 1953: Harold and Guy were both on
line when we heard the word. The 224th Regiment Battle

positions were in the Satae-ri and Sandbag Castle Sectors. The region of Kumwha Valley is changed forever.

Guns fell silent on July 27, 1953

Guy anticipated the results of the ongoing peace talks. In July 1953, a ceasefire agreement was made. This was just prior to Guy's twenty-first birthday. On July 26, 1953, we were notified of orders to cease fire the following day.

"No-man's land, a demilitarized zone, stretched two and a half miles wide across Korea. Evacuation was to be completed within seventy-two hours of the ceasefire. I don't know why seventy-two hours. I didn't see anybody alive on the other side of this line we were making. Evacuation was completed. I don't know what happened to the commanders and what they had to do with this area. During that waiting period of twenty-four hours, our unit took in more than 4,700 rounds of artillery fire. At 9:00 p.m. the night of July 28, 1953, all went silent" (**Guy Metcalf**).

Guy proudly served in Service Company 224th Infantry Regiment 40th Infantry Division in the Sandbag Castle area of Korea, somewhere north of Seoul. "This picture was taken the next day after the ceasefire went into effect at 9:00 p.m. on July 27, 1953. Our unit was in the process of pulling back the required one and a quarter miles called for by the truce and setting up the demilitarized zone. We placed signs such as the one in the picture to mark its boundaries. This was a great experience for a young soldier and was one of the happiest days of my young life" (**Guy Metcalf**).

Guy Metcalf at the demilitarized zone

The static line developed due to the ongoing negotiations by the United States and United Nations to enable a ceasefire. The commanders were not interested in battling for new territory but to maintain control of the areas that were secured. The only offensive action was to take and claim ground that was now held. Military command was reluctant to engage any new major battles. This type of operation would be classified as positional warfare: the use of force through tactics, firepower, or movement. Access was denied; we were merely to strengthen our positions and maintain subtle probes of the enemy's positions where they had sight advantage. There was a lot of artillery fire from both sides as an effort to solidify positions. The United States and the United Nations eventually negotiated a ceasefire that stopped where it began—at the 38th Parallel—the dividing line between North and South Korea.

The Korean War had stopped! Not a treaty of peace, but a pause in time. The conflict remained, the two sides—the isolated communist North and the capitalist South—were still at war. Peace talks brought stability and renewed hope for the future. I was so relieved to get out of there. The guns fell silent.

After the truce was signed, Guy and a detail of men were moving up online to pull back and create the no-man's land between North and South Korea. While driving along the road, he saw this soldier on the side of the road with a bandaged head injury. He did not converse with the soldier, but Guy Metcalf took the soldier's picture.

Unknown Soldier at the demilitarized zone

01 AUG 53 MOS CHANGED TO ORDERS FOR TDY

Get it while you can

Ten-minute break

04 AUG 53 HLM TDY TO WONJU—S&R 293RD QM GRAVES REGISTRATION COMPANY—8TH ARMY—ARRIVED YONG DONG PO—9:30 P.M.— AT YONG DONG PO—AUG 4–8

My orders changed, and I traveled for temporary duty to a Quarter Corps location in Wonju. Our section consisted of six men and a Korean interpreter to function as a search-and-recovery team (S&R) in the region. Wonju is now one of the most popular cities in Gangwon Province and was the site of three crucial battles during the Korea War known as the Battle of Wonju (first, second, and third). We traveled into the villages and communities questioning people. Carefully searching war-torn areas, we took a contoured detailed map of the area and would go grid by grid, searching foxholes and former battle sites in the attempt to locate any remains of American GIs, KIAs, and MIAs. We didn't have much success because that territory had been fought over so much. The missing remained just that. Search and recovery for KIAs of early battles of the war was a formidable task with very little success of locating the fallen.

S&R team—Ed Mullins, Fred Ellick, David Evans, and Harold Maples

Korean girl carrying a bundle on her head

The days were extremely cold. Mr. Lee, our interpreter, traveled with us on our daily mission. We became friends and were able to interact with the Korean villagers. They would invite us into their homes. This was my first up-close and face-to-face interaction with Korean citizens. Meeting Mr. Lee's family was an interesting cultural experience. Some rural Korean citizens had probably never seen an American GI before.

Consideration was always given to the land and the seasons prior to building houses in Korea because of the extreme weather conditions. Mr. Lee's home was carefully positioned and built against a hill facing south. As a result, his home got as much sunlight as was possible to warm his home. Korean homes still use an under-the-floor heating system, known as an *ondul*. The heat transferred from the wood heat warmed the underside of the floor of the home. Walls were of straw and mud, and the windows were wooden. As a result of the cultivation of rice, the byproduct (rice straw) was used for the straw-thatched roof and building material.

Korean home—Wonju

Wonju '53

Korean girl and boy

Korean home

C-rations, a staple of our military diet, included corned beef hash. We weren't always fond of corned beef, but the Korean families were. We took extra to share. In the cold weather, they heated the meal in a pot, along with their dried fish heads, which had a tremendous aroma.

Korean boys carrying a heavy load

Harold Maples

A common household drink, hot tea, was offered to Mr. Lee's guests to warm us from the inside. Made from fruits, leaves, seeds, and roots, the tea flavors could be salty, sweet, sour, bitter, and even pungent.

Rice is served often in Korea as a staple food, one of the main crops, along with barley, beans, and *Gochujang*, which is a hot pepper paste. Mr. Lee caught fish for his family, an important source of protein. The peninsula was home to many kinds of freshwater fish, including Korean taimen, Korean stumpy hopper, south torrent catfish, and the black shine.

Interpreter Lee, my friend

Carrying Lee in an A-frame

The interaction of Mr. Lee with our group was memorable. We relied on his knowledge and understanding of the Korean language and culture. Since the twentieth century, Korea has remained divided between the North and the South, resulting in many cultural differences.

Children could be seen in number. One day, these little kids were wading in the stream and taking a hammer, banging it against a rock, stunning the fish for catching. We had a good time joining them, kicking off our shoes, rolling up our pant legs, and wading in the stream. This was a way to get to know them better. Our interaction showed us that kids are kids, no matter the culture. Adults assumed the same fun role.

Lee with soldiers

Another time we walked down to the village to look around. Mama-san, a gentle lady, was selling jewelry on the sidewalk. She had these beautiful opal earrings that perhaps came out of China—well, nowadays everything does. I bought them for Phyllis and sent them home; quite a treasure and a memorable purchase.

Mama-san selling earrings

4/5 AUG 53 5TH ROK INFANTRY REGIMENT RELIEVED 224TH FROM SATAE-RI AND TOOK BIVOUAC POSITIONS AT TOKKOL-LI

06 AUG 53 224TH MOVED TO KUMWHA VALLEY

08 AUG 53 LEFT YONG DONG PO AT 12:15 P.M.— ARRIVED WONJU 5:45 P.M.

The Kim Story

Wonju had gotten back to some stability. Well after the truce was signed, communities were trying to get back to normal, to get on with their lives. Quonset huts were built for GI quarters. Now for a lighter side of war.

Accommodations were pretty good, and chow was much better, with some variety. We would go out during the daylight hours for search and recovery and come back to quarters at night. Some of the younger Korean men were used as house and errand boys. A most memorable experience of our brief time in Wonju was our houseboy, Kim. He was a young man who ran errands and did little things around the barracks. Learning Korean culture from our houseboy was an ongoing education.

My income was meager. I only kept two dollars out of each month's pay. I sent everything else I earned home to Phyllis. I didn't need money anyway. I would buy cigarettes for two dollars, though I didn't smoke. Kim would sell the cigarettes on the black market and make four dollars. I accumulated a little bit of cash this way. He was my go-between. I guess I didn't cheat the government out of too much. This allowed me to get enough money to send home Christmas gifts.

The Kim story is the upside of war-torn Korean romances. He informed us that he was to get married. This was a marriage arranged by his parents and grandparents, not something of his liking. Confucian values are at the center of traditional Korean holidays. The Happy Wedding, *Honrye,* is a union between families. Marriage is the most important passage of life. Prior to the blessed day, a great amount of time is spent matchmaking, called *Euihon,* arranged by the bride and groom's family.

Kim's comment in broken English: "I no wanta marry!" I asked, "Can I go to your wedding?" Kim's reply: "We don't have transportation." I jumped at this opportunity and asked, "If I get you transportation for family and guests, can I go?" Kim and I agreed that I would get the transportation, and I would be allowed to attend the wedding. Conversations with Kim at a later date indicated that the wedding would take place as planned. Knowing that this would be a once-in-a-lifetime experience to see an up-close Korean wedding, I seized upon that moment.

On the day of the wedding, I checked out a military vehi-cle—a two-and-a-half-ton truck with lots of seating space for hauling the Korean wedding party. Through the village I went, picking up lots of guests and family, then on to the wedding ceremony.

Korean taxi

A beautiful spring day for a wedding in Wonju, flowers were in vibrant bloom. I was fascinated by two roosters being held by two attendants. I'm not sure of the significance of the fowl to the ceremony; a symbol of a long and happy marriage, possibly.

The engaged couple wore traditional attire. Worn since ancient times, Mr. Kim's bride wore a *hanbok,* a traditional dress consisting of a jacket with long sleeves and a full wrap-around skirt. The colors were breathtaking—reds and yellows, including a white sash with flowers and red-crowned cranes. A knot was atop the bride's head for decoration. She wore boat-shaped shoes made of silk, with white cotton socks. Mr. Kim wore a jacket with loose sleeves, big trousers, and a black hat on his head.

Wedded bliss, the bride and groom

Becoming the wedding photographer was a special treat. Interrupting the ceremony was a challenge. I didn't understand that the groom and bride were not supposed to stand side by side for my photo—definitely a no-no! Since it had been an arranged marriage, I don't think the bride and groom had seen each other many times before the wedding. There was no physical contact during this stoic ceremony. That evening, I was able to attend the groom's bachelor party. It was a celebration of eating and toasting this most happy occasion. My military buddy and I attended the reception that evening. Singing was part of the reception, so they asked the two of us to sing a song. Surprisingly the only song we knew was "Good Night Irene." To say that it was amateurish would be a stretch.

Note the smiles with Kim, his beautiful bride, and their family and friends. Ceremonies are vastly different across cultures. Learning more about the Korean culture, so far removed from my own, was very interesting. Hopefully, the two are residing in Wonju and there is a house full of offspring.

Much like the following song by Edmund L. Gruber, our mission and routine activities continued on a daily basis:

"The Army Goes Rolling Along"

March along, sing our song, with the Army of the free,

Count the brave, count the true, who have fought to victory,

We're the Army and proud of our name,

We're the Army and proudly proclaim.

First Chorus:

First to fight for the right,

And to build the Nation's might,

And the Army Goes Rolling Along.

Proud of all we have done,

Fighting 'til the battle's won,

And the Army Goes Rolling Along.

Then it's Hi! Hi! Hey!

The Army's on its way,

Count off the cadence loud and strong.

For where e'er we go,

You will always know,

That the Army Goes Rolling Along.

Second Chorus:

Valley Forge, Custer's ranks,

San Juan Hill and Patton's tanks,

And the Army went rolling along.

Minutemen, from the start,

Always fighting from the heart,

And the Army keeps rolling along.

Third Chorus:

Men in rags, men who froze,

Still the Army met its foes,

And the Army went rolling along.

Faith in God, then we're right,

And we'll fight with all our might,

As the Army keeps rolling along.

Trio of Lee, Campbell, and Harold Maples

AUG 53 CHORWON VALLEY

08 NOV 53 R&R TOKYO—SEVEN DAYS AS A PFC

I received seven days of rest and relaxation (R&R) in Tokyo, Japan. I purchased a few Christmas presents with the little bit of money I had saved. One such gift was for an anticipated yet unborn daughter.

Porcelain Doll

Thoughts of home, my wife and son,

Longing, longing to join them,

Returning to the life I knew before,

Away from this desolate land and barren shore.

R & R to Japan to purchase a doll,

A beautiful, Porcelain Doll,

Carefully sending her home,

This delicate, fragile work of art,

How I yearn,

Hopeful to return.

Who is this gift of a beautiful porcelain doll for?

My unborn daughter, forevermore

—*Karen Maples Sams*—October 8, 2016

KAREN'S GISHA GIRL DOLL THAT
HAROLD BOUGHT IN JAPAN BEFORE
SHE WAS BORN

Porcelain Doll

16 DEC 53 LEFT WONJU FOR YOUNG DONG PO— RETURNING TO REGIMENT FROM TDY

17 DEC 53 LEFT YOUNG DONG PO

19 DEC 53 RETURNED FROM WONJU (PFC) TO CHORWON VALLEY—SERVICE COMPANY— CHRISTMAS 53 IN CHORWON VALLEY (CPL)

The truce now signed, we returned from Wonju to Chorwon Valley, collecting what few belongings we had, preparing to go home.

03 FEB 54 TDY SEOUL—BASKETBALL— FOURTEEN DAYS (CPL)—GROUP ACCUSED OF AWOL FROM THE COMPANY COMMANDER ALTHOUGH CLEARED TO TRAVEL BY HEADQUARTERS—TEAM RECEIVED FOURTEEN DAYS HARD LABOR FROM COMPANY COMMANDER—MADE SERGEANT WHILE GONE ON BASKETBALL TRIP—AWOL CORRECTED BY HDQ

Basketball

I heard about a basketball tournament in Seoul. For fun, a few of us decided we would put together a little basketball team, anything to escape the hills for a few days. Practice was limited, and we played outside on a dirt basketball court dressed in army fatigues and combat boots. Our team had only played one game. We were a sorry-looking lot; ragged was our fashionable look; bunker attire was the dress of the day.

Our orders to go were cleared through headquarters, and we were given a vehicle for transportation. We left the company and were now on our way to good quarters, tasty chow, and clothes. Man, we thought we were uptown! At departure, Corporal Montross was the ranking enlisted man in charge. The team of enlisted men of the 224th Infantry Regiment was placed on fourteen days TDY to Seoul on February 3, 1954, for practice and participation in the Division Basketball Tournament.

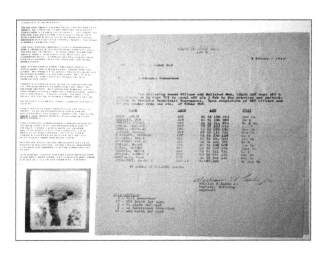

A chance at basketball

Tournament directors provided us with army-issued basketball shoes for the game. We were up against college graduate players and didn't last too long, but it was a good distraction and fun for us. The food and cherry pie were worth the trip. I wonder about these men on our basketball team. My hope and prayers are that they made it home safe to their families.

We came to a slight bump in the road. After our TDY to Seoul, we returned to the company area. We had been cleared for the trip by headquarters, but someone forgot to get word to our company commander. The orders had not been cleared through him. We were accused of being absent without leave (AWOL). While away, the rank came down, and I had been promoted to sergeant. I was not aware of this; thus, the commander held me responsible.

Five days later when we returned from Seoul, our commander met us, and shall we say, he was hot under the collar.

The company commander looked straight at me and said, "You are the one in charge." Being a three-week corporal, at that time, I didn't know how to respond. I just stood there and listened. He firmly reprimanded the entire basketball team and gave all of us fourteen days hard labor for being AWOL. This entailed cleaning stoves in the mess tent. Word got out to the company commander, and the orders were cleaned up. We got off hard duty after he found out what happened. I was absent without leave and promoted from PFC to sergeant rank all in the same day. Cheers! After making sergeant, my salary increased. I needed the extra dollars to send home.

Our basketball careers came to a sudden end. Graves Registration didn't have a lot to do since the truce had been signed. I was called in by the company commander. He said, "You get another stripe if you become mess sergeant." I was encouraged to go down to the mess hall and try it, even though I told him I couldn't cook. One day was my tenure. I skillfully recommended another guy who wanted the job. I made the decision to pass up this opportunity so I could apply for early release to return to my family and return to school at the University of Tennessee. I was ready to be home. Looking back on it, I realize I should have taken the opportunity of mess sergeant and gotten another stripe. I would have returned home and gone in the reserves. Not many could have gone from a slick sleeve except in a situation like that—getting sergeant first class in a matter of twenty months. Getting home soon was my priority.

Marilyn Monroe

Lucky for us, in February 1954, Marilyn Monroe and Joe DiMaggio were newlyweds on a trip to Japan. She decided to take a tour to Korea to entertain the troops. Twelve thousand soldiers braved the snow to see the popular actress on the outdoor stage. Marilyn owned the stage.

Our company was provided transportation to go to the show. Marilyn indicated that she was not as comfortable before a live audience as she was before cameras. She performed several songs and talked to the audience. Note that Marilyn's tour to entertain us was in February, a cold month in Korea. Marilyn wasn't clothed as well as the GIs she was entertaining. Her enduring the cold was quite a treat for us.

Marilyn Monroe entertaining the troops

Marilyn Monroe onstage

APR 54 TO INCHON FOR ROTATION HOME

08 MAY 54 THE 40TH DIVISION IN KOREA HELD A FINAL REVIEW WHERE PRESIDENT SYGMAN RHEE PRESENTED HIS PRESIDENTIAL UNIT CITATION—THE SUNBURST DIVISION MADE ITS LAST OFFICIAL APPEARANCE IN KOREA ON THIS DATE WHEN 8,500 SOLDIERS OF THE 110TH DIVISION PASSED IN A FAREWELL CEREMONY ON THE 40TH DIVISION PARADE GROUNDS. TOP ROK DIPLOMATIC AND MILITARY OFFICIALS LOOKED ON (GENERAL MAXWELL D. TAYLOR, 8TH ARMY COMMANDER)

17 MAY 54 ASCOM CITY—INCHON, SOUTH KOREA—PROCESSING FOR HOME

CHAPTER VI

SLOW BOAT HOME

Aboard the ship, home from the war,
Soon I will hold the one I adore;
My spirits are high, the voyage is long,
Back where I belong.
Karen Maples Sams *03/14/22*

02 JUN 54 BOAT TRIP FROM INCHON TO SAN FRANCISCO (1,600 HOUR SAIL—USNS WEIGEL—RETURNED TO CAMP STONEMAN, CALIFORNIA (NAVY TRANSPORT GENERAL WILLIAM WEIGEL) FLIGHT TO CAMP CHAFFEE

"During the Korean phase of her career, the *USS General William Weigel* sailed from the Pacific coast to Japan and Korea carrying troops for duty in the Korean War. She continued to rotate American troops to strengthen the United Nations position in Korea until she was placed in Reduced Operational Status in 1955."[4]

---

[4] http://en.wikipedia.org/wiki/USS_General_William_Weigel (AP-119)

USS *General William Weigel*

The slow boat home tells a unique story of soldiers on their journey home who survived the Korean War, soldiers who weren't sure they would see their families again. We were handed our papers to report for duty, and we served our country honorably and proudly, no questions asked.

Slow boat home

The trip home gave me a chance to reminisce, reflect, and relax for a job well-done. Reflecting back on the slow train ride from the Knoxville Railroad Station and how I ended up in this foreign land felt surreal. Our faces pressed hard up against the train windows to get a final glimpse of family. All felt similar feelings. Now, I shed tears of joy that I would soon be reunited with those I love.

The combat units and impatient soldiers were eager to board the *USS General William Weigel*. My division, the 40th, and the 45th Division were the first units to leave. We boarded the ship from Inchon to San Francisco, California. I was finally on my way home aboard the troop ship in April 1954. I got a clothing allowance and came home with the same shirt, pants, and shoes, nothing else; all issued clothing had to be turned in to supply.

This was an answer to all the prayers lifted up to bring us home safely. We had been counting down the days, the hours, the minutes. The anticipation and joy built. This would be one of my happiest moments.

16 JUN 54 BOAT DOCKED IN SAN FRANCISCO (FORT MASON BERTH)—155 OFFICERS ABOARD (SGT AND ABOVE)—ENLISTED MEN MOSTLY—11,000 MEN FOR PARADE—HLM WAITED UP ALL NIGHT FOR FLIGHT TO CAMP CHAFFEE, ARKANSAS

The boat docked in San Francisco, California, with a view of the Golden Gate Bridge. A lone ranger, we boarded an old DC 3 plane that brought us into Camp Chaffee, Arkansas. So much is taken for granted, it seems. Life is way too short to let days go by without sending a message to your loved ones that you love them. War is necessary, and I had no hesitation serving my country, a job to do; never forgetting those who sacrificed their lives. I dreamed of this day so many times—going home, no words. War controls your every waking moment. What we do for our country comes before our family, our jobs, our education. I returned home on Father's Day to a nine-month-old boy.

JUN 54 FATHER'S DAY—ARRIVED HOME

Lloyd is nine months old

Home

"The World had no room for cowards. We must all be ready somehow to toil, to suffer, to die. And yours is not the less noble because no drum beats before you when you go out to your daily battlefields. And no crowds shout you're coming when you return from your daily victory and defeat" (**Robert Louis Stevenson**).

"Growing up in the Depression, soldiers were from a time where you worked hard, no room for complaints or excuses. Soldiers came home quietly, picking up where they left off to provide for their families. They go to war for their country, saying little of their experience. My dad never talked much about the Korean War. I think it was too difficult, too painful to recall. He could never tolerate loud noises and is easily startled to this day. Watching the show *M*A*S*H* on a very small black-and-white television was my first look at the Korean War. A sit-com making a mockery of the war. It was all about playing doctor, drinking, fooling around, and cross-dressing as a way to get out of the army. Korean War soldiers had no choice. We could be under communist rule! South Korea would not exist! Parents, spouses, brothers, and sisters would welcome many veterans home with no banners, no parades, maybe an article in the newspaper" (**Karen Maples Sams**).

19 JUN 54 THE DIVISION'S COLORS AND BATTLE FLAGS WERE RETURNED TO CALIFORNIA AT A CEREMONY IN SAN FRANCISCO—UNIT

PARADED DOWN MARKET STREET AFTER THREE YEARS IN KOREA

The ceasefire influenced Guy's rotation and required him to remain in stateside service for six more months. After being in the contingent that brought the 40th's colors home, the army recalled the 40th Infantry Division to go back to California. Army buddy Guy Metcalf coincidentally returned to the States on the same ship, the *USS General William Weigel*. On his way back home, he too sailed into the San Francisco Bay.

"Eleven hundred strong, we were honored to bring the colors of the 40th Infantry Division and present them to the governor of San Francisco. A huge welcome-home party greeted us as we came down the gangplank. We led a huge parade down Market Street for four miles. We had many bands and dignitaries. A great turnout of people gathered along the parade route to cheer us on. The people of South Korea who we helped save from Communism are still very grateful today for the help we gave them. My Korean experience was tougher than I had anticipated, and it made a lifelong impression on my life. Not only did we fight the enemy, which turned out to be many Chinese, we fought the weather. Summers were blistering hot, and the winters were unbearably cold" (*Guy Metcalf*).

Guy values his experience and wouldn't trade it even if he could. Now South Korea ranks near the top of the most economically advanced nations in the world. Its development as a modern nation is due to the veterans who fought a treacherous ground war for democracy. In defense of this great country, the veterans of so many wars travel this voyage wearing a coat of many scars. Our minds are not able to break off from that journey, but eventually all journeys end in the same place: home!

09 JUL 54 CAMP CHAFEE, ARKANSAS—GREYHOUND TO KNOXVILLE

10 JUL 54 DISCHARGE FROM ACTIVE DUTY

"To this day my Dad has never slept through the night. He is easily startled when approached while awake or asleep. Noises still impact him. Fireworks on the Fourth of July and loud noises make him jump, along with others approaching him unannounced" (***Karen Maples Sams***). Harold was relieved of active duty in July 1954 at the rank of sergeant and was awarded the Korean Service Medal (KSM) with two Bronze Stars (BSS), the United Nations Service Medal (UNSM), Combat Infantry Badge (CIBAD) and two Overseas Services (O/S) Bars; also the National Defense Service Medal (NDSM), Republic of Korea (ROK), Presidential Unit Citation (PUC), and Good Conduct Medal (GCM). His unit was on Sandbag on that eventful day of ceasefire on July 27, 1953.

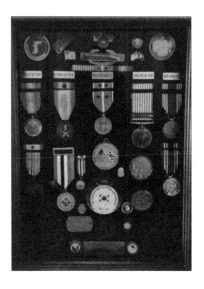

Korean War medals

11 AUG 54 READY RESERVES

The Badge of Glory

Of all the medals upon our chests,

From battles of war, we knew;

The one admired as the very best,

Is the one of infantry blue.

It's only a rifle upon a wreath,

So why should it mean so much?

It is what it took to earn it,

That gives it that magic touch.

To earn the special accolade,

You face the enemy's fire;

Whether you survived or not,

God dialed that one desire.

For those of us who served the cause,

And brought the nation glory;

It's the Combat Infantryman's Badge,

That really tells the story (***Unknown Author***).

Home sweet home! Back to life as we knew it. Those who came back went over as clerks, farmers, auto mechanics, teachers—a diverse group of proud individuals. When we came back, we didn't expect anything. You just did a job for your country.

Now a reality, I returned home a different person—more mature, more humble, and more grateful. I never looked at my life the same after the Korean War. Going back to the life I knew before was a challenge. It seemed impossible to step from the battlefield to civilian life as the same person, but I did it. I was changed forever.

Home sweet home

Powell Station gate

The home loans we received for our military service were tremendously helpful. Another was the financial aid from the GI Bill for college and supplemental veteran benefits. Against all odds and with help from Phyllis, I continued my college education. Surprising myself, I graduated with a Bachelor of Science degree in education. I used my degree to establish a career as a physical director at the Young Men's Christian Association (YMCA) and pioneering the sport of scuba diving (SCUBA) in East Tennessee. Our dive shop was C/I Underwater Activities, located near downtown Knoxville. I later worked as the assistant director of admissions at the University of Tennessee in undergraduate admissions.

Hills of Tennessee

Many years later, well into my eighties, 2018 to be exact, I received additional Veteran Administration benefits for my hearing loss. This was surprising because all I did was apply for hearing aids. Not only did I get the hearing aids I desperately needed, but the Veterans Administration also determined that my hearing loss was 100 percent, a result of the war. Military benefits fully compensated for the cost of the hearing aids and some back pay. I was provided a new pair of hearing aids, which were much more comfortable, and they allowed me to hear a little better. Now in my nineties in 2022, I qualified for cochlear hearing aid implants. Amazingly, I can now hear when others speak and when music is played. I will be able to experience the joy of hearing my great-grandchildren.

"At the war's conclusion more than 33,600 United States military personnel were listed as killed in action, and over 2,700 had died in captivity. Approximately 8,000 Americans were listed missing in action and 103,000 wounded" (***Unnamed Korean War Veteran***).

Rice paddy fields—Yanggu Pass

Howard Hinkle and Harold Maples

CHAPTER VII

HONORING ALL VETERANS—
EVERYONE HAS A STORY TO TELL

V eterans of the Korean War who I met through the Korean War Veteran Association (KWVA), regimental reunions, dedication ceremonies, and email communications have a story to tell and encouraged me to write down some of their experiences. They were dedicated to the cause and created an unforgettable friendship. Their stories contributed greatly to the contents of this book, also the insight about serving for the preservation of freedom and noting the evacuation of the wounded, those not accounted for. The mortally wounded in body bags sacrificed their lives for their country.

"The Battle of Kapyong took place from April 22 to April 25 , 1951 during the Korean War. The actions of the 2nd Battalion, Princess Patricia's Canadian Light Infantry (PPCLI) and the 3rd Battalion, Royal Australian Regiment were critical in preventing a breakthrough against the United Nations central front, the encirclement of United States forces in Korea and ultimately the capture of Seoul. They bore the entire brunt of the assault and stopped an entire Chinese People's Volunteer Army division estimated at 10,000–20,000 in strength during the hard-fought defensive battle."[5]

Kapyong High School

Always leave things better off than when you found them. The story goes something like this: Kapyong High School was built by the Ball of Fire Construction Corps. The school was envisioned by Major General Joseph P. Cleland, division commander and project engineer. It was erected with donations from the 40th Division personnel. Brigadier General Rogers was also a project engineer, and Captain W. M. H. Yates was the architect. Stockholders consisted of 40th Division citizens of Kapyong. Equipment and medicine were purchased in Japan by Lieutenant Leonard Lewis. A modern dispensary is the latest addition to the Kenneth Kaiser High School at Kapyong. Additional money was raised to sustain the medical dispensary. The medical unit meets the needs of many students.

After seeing the lack of schooling facilities for the many children displaced by the Kapyong Battle, the men of the 40th Division stationed in Korea turned their attention to the plight of the Korean people. Korean citizens worked to provide schooling in makeshift conditions. Under the leadership of General Cleland, the men of the 40th took it upon themselves to finance the project with GI donations to erect a school building. Both young and old donated to the cause. Soldiers reached into their pockets and wrote home

---

[5]   http://en.m.wikipedia.org/wiki/Battle_of_Kapyong

to families and friends for money and clothing to assist the orphanages and the community.

Today, Kapyong High School is one of the largest academic standard schools in South Korea, graduating outstanding students. A worthwhile project, the United States soldiers built the Kenneth Kaiser Memorial High School in honor and memory of the first man in the 40th Division (the Fireball Division) to lose his life in the Korean Conflict, Sergeant Kenneth Kaiser. Sergeant Kaiser was with Company B 160th Infantry Regiment of the 40th Division when he was killed on January 20, 1952. The memorial plaque stands to this day.

Ball of Fire—Kapyong High School

The Kaiser School is the first co-educational high school in Korea. There were many other units that adopted projects and villages to rebuild what the up-and-down military action had destroyed. The lingering thought is that the US troops fought for the Korean people in war and provided for them in the aftermath. The Kapyong High School represents a proud remembrance of United States soldiers attempting to bring back some order to the lives of children in the Kapyong Village.

Papa-san—Kapyong High School

All an American serviceperson ever wants is to preserve our faith, liberty, and way of life, and to remember those who gave their lives for the preservation—but yet we hear from some and the media the loud echo of "Yankee, go home!" Kapyong High School is still in existence today and of service to the Kapyong Village.

Wartime Pets

It was not unusual for Korean veterans to adopt stray pets. Our Graves Section adopted a mixed-breed dog. We quickly named her C-ration and her puppy Digger. My friend Guy was able to provide some food for the dogs since he was stationed in ration breakdown. I was placed on TDY for a period of time and never learned the fate of the pets. Consumption of dog meat is common in Korea, and it was eaten during the Boknal Festival. The festival commemorates the hot summer months in South Korea with the consumptions of various stews, a tradition on special occasions. This is now a declining, illegal practice and is being closed down.

Harold Maples and C-ration

Digger

Nick Spartichino's Introduction to the Army

"Harold, I'm going to write about my time in the service. I think it would be interesting for my grandchildren to know something about the history of their granddad. You may print anything that may be of use to you.

"It all started on January 2, 1953, when I was to report to south Boston for the physical that I passed. It was located on the second floor of the building. I think that if you made it up the flight of stairs, you were accepted into the army. Later we were loaded on a bus and driven to Fort Devens, located in Ayer, Massachusetts. Arriving at nighttime, it was very cold. We were taken to a barrack, which was unheated. It was just as cold as outside. We stayed in there so long we thought they had forgotten about us. They finally took us to a heated barrack. We stayed at Fort Devens for six days, and during that time, we were issued our uniforms and given a very close haircut. We engaged in some physical training (PT) and taught close order drills. We were then told the different basic training camps that we were going to. I was assigned to Indian Town Gap, located in Pennsylvania. We were loaded into a bus for the long ride. When we arrived, we were to fall in, and we were given the rules. We were then told to go into the barracks and put on our field equipment and then fall out.

Nick Spartichino in Chorwan Valley

"I went outside, and I was all by myself. The company commander, Lieutenant Goss, came out. He told me when I went back to the barracks that I was to take the first bunk on the right. That was the squad leader's bunk. The good part of being a squad leader was that for the next four long months I only had kitchen police (KP) once.

"After basic training we had a short leave before we were to report to the army base in New York for a few days. From there, we went by bus to the ship for the long voyage. The name of the ship was the Marine Carp. The ship was built for the Atlantic Ocean; therefore, it did not have air-conditioning, something we would have appreciated on the hot days ahead on the Pacific Ocean" (**Nick Spartichino**).

"The *USNS Marine Carp* was a Marine Adder-class transport that saw service with the United States Navy for the task of transporting troops to and from combat areas. She was of the C4-S-A3 design type, built for the United States Maritime Commission (MARCOM) during World War II and the Korean War. The ship earned the Korean Service

Medal (KSM). Established November 8, 1950, by executive order from Harry S. Truman, the ship won a military award for service or participation during operation in the Korean War between June 27, 1950 and July 27, 1954."[6]

USNS *Marine Carp*

"We set sail in the middle of May, the same day we boarded the ship. Some had duty on the ship; my luck was to report for KP every other day. Others were lucky and had no chores. We were given quarters for sleeping. The bunks were pipes with canvas stretched across them, with rope stacked four high when lying down. Your face was only inches from the bunk above.

"On the ship we were expected, upon waking, to make our bed, get cleaned up, clean around our bed, then go and have chow. After chow, we were to remain on deck until the cabins were inspected.

---

[6]   http://en.m.wikipedia.org/wiki/USNS_Marine_Carp (T-AP-199)

"Our first stop was Puerto Rico. We had some Korean War vets on board going home. We were allowed to leave the ship to go to the post exchange (PX). The air was so humid the glue on our mail envelopes stuck together. When we returned, they loaded around 500 Puerto Rican soldiers aboard ship. We were there about three days, then we left for Colombia to get Colombian soldiers. We were there for six hours before heading to the Panama Canal. As luck would have it, I was on KP, so I didn't get to see much of it. While on KP, we felt a bump. I went up on deck to see what had happened. Going through the locks, the ship rubbed against the heavy wood lining on the side of the lock. It was still smoking from the friction.

"That night we were allowed to leave the ship but had to stay within sight of it. On land, there were small, almost like telephone booths selling beer. I bought one and sat down under a palm tree to enjoy it. Some had as much beer as they could before going back on board. A few soldiers were so drunk, they were climbing the anchor chain to get back on board.

"Next stop was the Hawaiian Islands. On the way there, we had a little excitement. We ran into a monsoon. The bow of the ship would sink into the ocean, and the spray would come halfway to the back of the ship. Needless to say, we got soaked. So, we had a really good look at the fury of the monsoon. We were only in Hawaii for six hours to get fuel and provisions. We were let off the ship to watch a show in a warehouse where the entertainment was a stage performance of some girls in sarongs dancing, a welcome sight for a change.

"After leaving Hawaii, our next stop was to the island of Sasabo, Japan. Upon arrival we went to the warehouse to get our combat gear and rifles. I was overwhelmed with the number of M1 rifles. There were pallets as far as I could see, stacked with more than 100 rifles per pallet. The M1 rifle is a semiautomatic rifle that was the United States' service rifle during World War II and the Korean War.

"Immediately after, we headed back to the ship and onto our new destination of Inchon, Korea. We arrived on the Fourth of July and could hear the artillery from our position. We were stuck in the harbor for three days because of the thick fog. The fourth day was still foggy, but we got off the ship and onto landing crafts. On our way to Korea, we were packed like sardines, standing room only with our gear, including duffle bags. The pilot could not see the shore. I don't think he even knew how to read a compass. He lucked out finding shore. This ended the long voyage of forty-one days.

"When we reached the shore, we were loaded onto eighteen-wheeler open trucks for the ride to the railroad station. A train was waiting for us. We boarded an old train with wooden seats for a long ride to the repo depot. Our backsides were sore by the time we arrived.

"Upon arrival, we were assigned to our outfits. I was to go to the 40th 224th Infantry Division. While there, a medical officer, Lieutenant Semiday (who also happened to be in charge of sporting events), said, 'You look like you can box. Would you like to give it a try?' I said, 'Why not?' The next day I was in the ring for the first time. My opponent was a tall guy with the longest arms I had ever seen. He beat me so badly, the referee asked if I wanted to go on. Yes, he beat the living hell out of me. That was the end of my boxing career.

Guard Duty

"We moved by truck from the Kumwah Valley to Chorwon Valley. We arrived late at night and relieved a Greek outfit. We were escorted to the trench line. You could not see your hand if it was in front of your face. We were feeling our way along the trench line. With each step, we heard a crunching sound every time we put our foot down. We slept in our pup tents that night. In the morning, we found out what the crunching noise was. There was a migration of frogs earlier that night, and they fell into the trench line. There were snakes that followed them; they fell in also. That day we had to shovel them out.

"I was led to what was now my bunker. The Browning Automatic Rifle (BAR) remained on line at all times. That day we were putting up squad tents. My hands were so sweaty from the heat that they kept slipping when we were trying to put up the main poles, so I took my belt off and wrapped it around the pole. It was working well until it broke. After the tents were up, we got the news that we were going to the shower. We boarded trucks to the shower point. There we turned in our old, smelly clothes, took a quick shower, and were given clean clothes. When I put the pants on, they were so large Jackie Gleason could have gotten in with me. Don't forget I had no belt. When we got back to the squad, we got off the truck. Guess what happened when I jumped off the truck?

"Chorwon Valley was the only thing between the Chinese and us, flat land for at least a mile. We had a tank moving back and forth, setting off booby traps in front of our position in preparation for us to lay barbed wire. The closer the enemy got to us, the narrower the wire got, leading the enemy into fire from machine guns, our BARs. This was done in the rainy season. The water was about four inches high. While laying the wire, I broke two trip wires. You could not see them because they were underwater. I don't know what they were attached to; they must have been old and rusty.

"We went to the supply room for ammunition and flak jackets. We were told we would be staying there overnight before going on line. They also told us they were expecting a concentrated artillery bombardment over a wide area, known as a barrage. We were told where to go if this happened. We slept on duffle bags for a bed that night. The next morning, we were taken to the command post for orientation, then on to the front line. I was told which bunker I was to go to. It was small, but it did have homemade bunks made from tree limbs and wire over cardboard for a mattress. With the flak jacket on, it wasn't too uncomfortable.

"I was placed in the second squad under squad leader Sergeant Sproul, a nice guy. My first job was in a bunker that had a board with battery leads to five-gallon cans. These cans contained napalm jellied gasoline and were placed at different locations. Each terminal was marked for each can. The slope that the bunker was on was very steep. I don't know how anybody could climb up it. Except for a few mortar rounds, it was calm. I had bunker guard duty that night. The seat on it was made out of steel. The part that I sat on was a steel circle with an overseas cardboard top; it was very uncomfortable.

"I was to report to the command post and was informed that I had been chosen to leave Korea early, as I was going to be part of a contingent bringing the colors back to California and return the 40th Division back to the states. We left by plane to Japan and then onboard the *USS General William Weigel* for a two-week trip back to the States.

"We approached the Golden Gate Bridge in the morning. The bridge looked like it was made out of pure, shiny gold. It was so bright it made your eyes squint—so beautiful. I now know how the bridge got its name.

"We took a ferry boat to an army base, staying there for a few days training to march down Market Street to the capital to return the division to Governor Knight, if memory serves me right. We boarded a plane back to the East Coast, and after a short leave I was to go to Fort Dix, New Jersey. I was made an assistant drill instructor for the rest of my stay in the United States Army and was discharged on January 2, 1955. Writing my story down helped me realize how much I have forgotten. Harold, don't forget I started this for you to use as you please and ended up writing this as a history for my kids" (***Nick Spartichino***).

Leo Bromleny's training was different, with its own unique challenges. His story follows:

"In May of 1953, we were at Fort Lewis about three days before boarding a troop ship en route to Sasebo, Japan, and our temporary quarters were at a former Japanese naval base. Most GIs remember their ship cruises and will most likely describe them in very frank terms. It was one hell of a ride—seasick, hanging out over the bunk, the various stenches, and diesel fuel. I often wonder why they did not issue military medals for this experience!

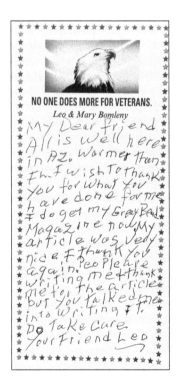

NO ONE DOES MORE FOR VETERANS.

Leo & Mary Bomleny

My Dear Friend All is well here in AZ. Warmer than Fl. I wish To Thank you for what you have done for me. I do get my GrayBeard Magazine now My article was Very nice. I Thank you again. People are writing me I think me for the article but you talked me into writing it. Do Take Care. Your Friend Leo

Leo's note

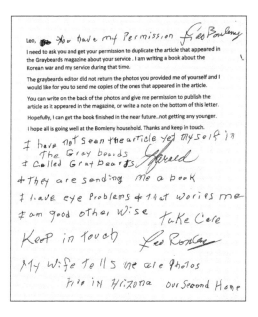

Leo's note to Harold

"To say I was very sick is an understatement. I stayed in my bunk for two days, avoiding food. After two days I felt somewhat better, and I ventured out to the chow line. From a farmer's perspective, the line resembled cattle-like feed troughs with a slide on them in order to help you hold on and chase your food tray. This went on for approximately two weeks.

"After this extreme survival experience ended, I arrived in Sasebo, where I stayed for several days while awaiting orders to Korea. We stayed busy spending our time being issued our M1 rifles and clothing, test firing at the range and listening over and over to the instruction, 'Don't forget to clean your weapons.' Finally, we went to the docks at Sasebo for the boat ride to Pusan, Korea.

"My experiences really began at the landing in Pusan. As this is written, I ask myself, 'Do you jot things down as a way to remember or a way to forget?' Most Korean War veterans would probably say that their service duty was a turning point in their lives. In the case of Korea, this was the start of a forward direction for the South Korean people who have become a thriving society. Those were people we hardly knew.

"Upon our arrival at Pusan, we marched to a small train with park bench–type seats, under which were stored cases of GI ammo prepped for easy breakout. Every third car was a flatbed with sandbag-fortified 30-caliber machine guns. The troops were loaded and headed north on a double-track railroad. Trains going north were carrying wounded troops. We could see them on the passing train cars. This gave each of us an eerie feeling as to what lay ahead. We were getting a view of war at ground level, noting destroyed cities and refugee villages.

Airplanes flew behind SFC Leo Bromleny, Fox Company 40th Division in the Punch Bowl

"We traveled north to a replacement depot near Seoul, Korea. We stayed in Seoul several days, until a division or company requested needed replacements. Fox Company of the 224th Infantry Regiment of the 40th Division needed me, and off I went, traveling by truck to an area known as the Punch Bowl, where the road ended. We walked the remaining distance to the trenches and the comfort of bunker living near Haean-Myeon Valley, a township in South Korea. Seeing the trenches and bunkers made me reflect on what World War I and II warfare must have been like.

"As members of Fox Company, we stayed in the Punch Bowl area for several weeks, then we moved and took up positions at Satae-ri. This is where I saw navy planes coming over our positions and dropping napalm on the enemy, many of whom were bathed in flames. That forced them out in the open for easy targeting by our machine gunners and mortars. This is where war came to life for me.

"Static and positional machine gun fights were constant and common to the Korean War actions at that time. Frequent patrols were part of the action. We were worn out as the Fourth of July approached, which was a day I will never forget.

"Somehow tracer ammo of all colors became available from the communists' machine guns. They fired rounds that lit up the sky and landscape. Lots of firing took place. Seeing extensive enemy tracer fire on July 4 made me wonder if this could have been mocking fire, considering our country's annual Fourth of July celebration.

"Satae-ri is the area where we suffered through a big battle on our final night of the fighting. Both sides fired most of the ammunition at one another. Our machine gun was hit and blown up on top of me. Our bunker was shot up badly from mortar and artillery fire. The battle was so intense I felt that I was surely going to die! Prayers were on my lips all during this intensification. Suddenly, around 10:00 p.m., all went silent along the front.

Trenches at Satae-ri Valley

"An urgent rush began to pull back and move all personnel, equipment, and weaponry south from the front to the back. No-man's land was drawn by stringing barbed wire. Just prior to the ceasefire, in an effort to use all available ammo, all weapons were being fired to quell an enemy barrage that was all along our regimental front. It was similar to fireworks on the Fourth of July that night. Seeing how many rounds you can get rid of on both sides of the line. We just had to clean house.

"The rest of the day and into the night of the ceasefire was filled with lots of firing on both sides. Both sides were seemingly saying that no one wants to carry out a lot of ammo, so keep your heads down and fire at will. The last mortar round was reloaded and fired at 9:45 p.m. On that eventful day of July 27, 1953, at 2200 hours, 10:00 a.m. Korean time, an eerie silence fell across the front. The fog lifted, and out of the smoke came the ceasefire. A few rounds came in, but thankfully no one was hurt. On the last day of action, the enemy fired in 4,799 rounds at the 40th Division and got better than 11,000 in return. The troops were a busy bunch completing the task of the evening on July 30, 1953. There was not a lot of ammunition to tote out of the no-man's land. I wonder who was doing the counting.

"I suffered a head wound on August 29, 1953, which, I learned later, might have resulted from sniper fire a month after the ceasefire went into effect. I woke up covered in blood. Two soldiers took me down the mountain to the medic's tent. The medic flipped the scalp over the wound, stapled it, and wrapped the wound. The guys took me back to my tent. The heavily bandaged wound made it difficult for me to wear headgear. As a result, my duty assignment was changed. I was assigned to work in the mess hall. The new job worked out great for me. I was an old farm boy, and I knew how to cut meat and cook. My wound healed gradually in about twenty days. I was able to do more work and accept more responsibility. Later, I was promoted to mess sergeant.

"We stayed hunkered down in an eerie quiet until daylight. That morning I looked toward the enemy positions and saw five or six women wearing bright-colored clothing coming down the mountain on the enemy's side. I guess they were coming to greet us! They knew the firing was over. Our orders were to pull back and to make no contact with our incoming visitors. One can only guess as to the visitors' motives.

"It wasn't long before it was time for me to go home. I rode into Inchon on a truck to begin the journey home. My Korean War duty was over. The return voyage to Seattle, Washington, via troopship made me realize what happy truly meant. The ride home was better than the one going over. I did not lose my cookies once. When we arrived at Seattle, I boarded a train to Chicago and received a thirty-day leave, after which I reported to Fort Carson Army Base in Colorado for separation. From there it was back home to the farm, under the cows, doing what I had been doing before I left.

"For all of my GI friends who have been there and done that—cheers! Thank you to anyone who may have served in Fox Company" (**Leo Bromleny**).

In Retrospect, Honoring PFC Robert Bernier

Sergeant Spartichino confirmed the name of PFC Robert Bernier, and the Regimental Parade Field was named in Robert's honor. The same field was mentioned on the web pages by family members. Nick provided a copy of the picture.

"Robert was from Massachusetts, in Suffolk County. He served in the United States Army, 224th Infantry Regiment, 40th Infantry Division specializing in light weapons assault crewman during the Korean War. Private Bernier faced his death on July 26, 1953, as a KIA in action hostility in North Korea. He was awarded the Purple Heart."[7]

---

[7] http://www.koreanwar.org/html/2110/korean-war-project-massachusetts-us51214051-pvt-robert-walter-bernier).

Ironic that you get information shifted between veterans so many years later. That was the last KIA from hostile action. Prior to the ceasefire, we had others who had accidents. I always think about the last casualty every July 27. What if Robert had been issued a flak jacket? I think of Robert and his family. It's something you will never erase from your mind. It's impossible. The ones who didn't make it home, who lost their lives, the soldiers we cannot locate are just sacrifices they endured for everybody else.

There is no comparison to the pain and suffering of prisoners of war (POWs) and those missing in action (MIA). "Adopted in 1972, the National League of Families POW/ MIA flag is often referred to as the POW/MIA flag. The design is a silhouette of a POW before a guard tower and barbed wire in white on a black field. POW/MIA appears above the silhouette, and the words 'You Are Not Forgotten' appear below in white on the black field."[8]

POW/MIA

---

[8] https://en.wikipedia.org/wiki/National_League_of_Families_POW/ MIA_Flag

The Search for Peace Continues

The war between the two Koreas started and ended where it began: at the 38th Parallel. It reached international proportions, and at least 2.5 million lives were lost from 1950 to 1953. The commencement of aggression seems to have started from the Union of Soviet Socialist Republics (USSR) wanting to increase the spread of Communism. Russia was responsible for the advisement and backing of North Korean forces that streamed across the 38th Parallel on June 25, 1950, meeting very little resistance from South Korea.

Historians are still trying to determine who started the conflict. The accomplishment was the prevention of Communism taking over South Korea, the testing of President Harry Truman's determination and the United States involvement.

The casualty report proves to be an ongoing update of the number of soldiers who died in the war zone from battle, illness, accidents and non battle causes. They died in captivity and others are missing in action. The search continues to locate and identify those unaccounted for to bring them home.

KWLF presentation by Samantha Fraser

The armistice ended the fighting, but sporadic outbreaks of violence exist to this day along the monitored demilitarized zone (DMZ). The DMZ is a buffer zone that extends about 160 miles across the two Koreas. This resulted in the deaths of United States and the Republic of Korea military personnel. Families are still split, with many never seeing their relatives again. South Korea, a thankful nation, has risen from the ashes of war to become a most prosperous nation and is an example of how freedom works. The search for peace continues.

What Happened to My Army Buddy?

"Have you ever wondered what happened to your army buddy that you knew in the early '50s, or wish you could find those guys, talk with them about old times, and perhaps share old pictures or other memorabilia?" (*Ron Gorrell*).

Ron Gorrell made the above comment about his mission, and he founded the 224th Infantry Association. He organized the first nationwide reunion for all the 224th Infantry coast-to-coast. Many Korean War, 224th Infantry veterans are very grateful for his efforts. The following is the listing of many joyous reunion occasions that Phyllis and I were able to attend.

Dates of the 224th Infantry Gallahad Regiment Reunions

1996 Ontario, California
1998 Colorado Springs, Colorado
2000 Washington, DC
2002 San Antonio, Texas
2004 Ventura, California
2006 St. Louis, Missouri
2008 Seattle, Washington
2009 Boston, Massachusetts
2010 Jacksonville, Florida
2011 Phoenix, Arizona

Ron went to great lengths to locate all 224th members and organize reunions. The first reunion was in Ontario, California, in 1996. During the Korean Government Arizona reunion, the consulate member presented Ambassador of Peace Medals to all members in attendance. "We now have over 1,100 Galahad veterans" (*Ron Gorrell*).

Combat Wounded Veterans Monument, November 11, 2011

"Many Korean War veterans never received a national parade when they returned from the battlefront. Instead, they quietly returned to their lives. The war receded from popular memory. Not so for the 600-plus current members of the 224th Infantry Regiment, 40th Infantry Division. Every eighteen months, they gather to remember" (***Ray Fanning***).

The 224th Infantry Regiment Association reunions have since ended. Our last time together was held in Phoenix, Arizona, on November 11, 2011. Note this special date being 11/11/2011—a fitting day for a military reunion. The date is quite visible on the side of the trolley.

Galahad Korean War veterans—Phoenix, Arizona

Honoring All Veterans

"Honor is overdue for Korean War veterans' service. Many years ago, representatives of the United Nations, North Korea, and China signed an armistice agreement in the tiny village of Panmunjom, South Korea, ending hostilities in the Korean War. Nearly 5 million people had perished during the previous three years, almost 40,000 of them Americans. The first military action of the Cold War, however, still shadows life on the Korean Peninsula, and its geopolitical ramifications are still felt today.

"In the United States, the conflict is often referred to as the Forgotten War. It was sandwiched between World War II, which united the nation more than any other event in our history, and the Vietnam War, the most divisive event since the Civil War. The Korean conflict cannot be overlooked. But for the men and women who served in Korea, and to their families, the war left an indelible mark on their lives. Congress made no formal war declaration. Seventy-five thousand Soviet-equipped North Korean troops poured over the 38th Parallel, which was where the allies divided Korea at the end of World War II.

"The North Koreans quickly captured Seoul and occupied much of the South until General Douglas MacArthur ordered an amphibious landing at Inchon that turned the tide. The United Nations forces, primarily made up of American and South Korean troops, then swept into North Korea. Feeling its southern frontier threatened, China sent troops in support of North Korea and pushed back the United Nations and South Korean forces. Once the front stabilized near the 38th Parallel in the summer of 1951, the war turned into a bloody slugfest and ended with a ceasefire that essentially restored the pre-war border.

"The soldiers and sailors of the Korean War who have submitted the vignettes tell the story of a different war, the real one that Hollywood has never depicted. It was a war of vicious firefights in frigid weather against a tenacious foe that gave no quarter and expected none. They endured unspeakable horrors unimaginable to civilians here at home.

"In the decades since the ceasefire was signed at Panmunjom, South Korea has grown into an economic powerhouse, a modern, industrialized, wealthy nation. North Korea, on the other hand, has shriveled into poverty and isolation, one of the last remaining outposts of Communism.

"Technically, the Korean conflict has not ended. The ceasefire never was followed by a peace treaty. The opposing armies still face one another across the demilitarized zone established by the armistice. North Korean dictator Kim Jong-un, grandson of the first North Korean strongman, Kim Il-sung, has continued the family tradition of saber-rattling. His saber, however, has a nuclear tip. Tensions remain high. Containing North Korea remains an American foreign policy goal after many decades.

"They may have fought in the'"Forgotten War,' but veterans of the Korean conflict belatedly are being recognized as they enter their twilight years. HonorAir, the organization run by Knoxville businessman Eddie Mannis, flies Korean War veterans to Washington, DC, to see the nation's memorials. They earned our appreciation and respect decades ago in the mountains of the Korean peninsula and in the waters offshore. No matter how much time has passed, and regardless of how much more attention other conflicts receive, their service and sacrifice cannot be forgotten" (***Author Unknown***).[9]

Recognition Well Deserved

After the Korean War, we faded into the mainstream of American life, keeping memories to ourselves. Wednesday, October 1, 2014, marked a unique perspective for Guy and me. We shared an HonorAir flight to Washington, DC, along with other Korean War Veterans, to view the lasting memorials dedicated to American service members.

The irony of this situation is that the HonorAir flight provided us the opportunity to once again board another shared flight. March 17, 1953, was our first shared flight, and originated from Sea Island Airport, Vancouver, Canada, en route to the Far East Command. Our time lapse between military flights was sixty-plus years; therefore, there is some irony in the two differing flight schedules.

---

[9] **Knoxville News Sentinel, July 28, 2013**

Guy and I shared the rugged, mountainous terrain of North Korea, following each other all the way through service. We would quickly learn that our journey would completely change our lives forever. It would create a new approach to life and death.

We both give thanks to the organization of HonorAir and the relentless effort from chairman Eddie Mannis and his volunteer staff. This provided World War II and Korean War veterans the opportunity to share an unforgettable day together. It provided two journeying soldiers an opportunity to share the visualization of the nineteen poncho-clad bronze soldiers of the Korean War Memorial. The chiseled faces of the patrol speak volumes; seeing the statues up close leaves a lasting impression.

HonorAir Flight

"Here are my favorite veterans: Harold Maples, my grand-father, and his friend, Guy Metcalf. They served in the Korean War together and have amazing stories to tell. Honor your veterans by listening to their stories. They deserve your time, plus they are just awesome people" (*Samantha Fraser— November 11, 2014*).

Congressman Joe Duncan greeting the HonorAir flight attendees— Amanda Cate, Guy Metcalf, Joe Duncan, Harold Maples, and Alvin Webb

Letter from Eli to Harold Maples:

September 14, 2014

Dear Mr. Maples,

My name is Eli. I am in the fifth grade. I like to play sports. I like basketball, football, and baseball. When I grow up, I want to be a gym teacher. I love Subway. I also love riding my four-wheeler. I am a Christian who loves God. I am looking forward to learning about World War II and the Korean War.

I thank you for your help and hard work. If you didn't do what you did, our country would not be the wonderful place it is today. Thank you. What branch of the military did you serve in? Again, thank you for what you did for me and many other people. *Your friend, Eli*

Response letter to Eli from Harold Maples:

Dear Eli,

Thanks a bunch for your really neat letter that was given to me on the HonorAir flight to Washington, DC. That was a real surprise, especially to receive the letter from someone living in Corryton. I have friends there: the Longmires and others. Be sure to give my thanks to your teacher for the goodie bag and the support. You are to be congratulated as a fifth grader who has set some great goals for your future. As for the four-wheeler, keep it upright!

I served in the United States Army during the Korean War, and our unit was on line during the signing of the cease-fire treaty. I was able to return home to my wife and nine-month-old son and continue my education at the University of Tennessee. For your information, I majored in education, physical education, and educational psychology. You go big time for your teaching goal—aim high in life—and meet the challenges!

Thanks again for your letter,
Harold Maples
P.S. Have a sub with your best school pal!

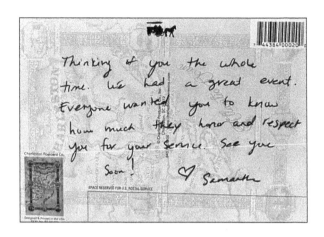

Sam's Note

My great-granddaughter, Sylvia, was five years old when she wrote this letter. Her school, Dunaway Elementary, celebrated and honored veterans by making cards and gaining a better understanding of what service to our country means.

"Our kindergarten friends wanted to be sure and thank you for your service! Today, to celebrate YOU, we watched an amazing *Salute to the Armed Forces* on YouTube and felt patriotic and proud! We also explored, in our weekly *Scholastic News Weekly Reader,* the work servicemen and -women do! Enjoy reading your cards!"

The inside of Sylvia's card reads:

Didi, "You keep us safe. You are a hero. Today is your day."
Thank you, Sylvia 11/11/2018

Kelly's Story

"Growing up, Mimi and Didi's place was a second home for me. I spent weekends and holidays in Powell, Tennessee, and summers on the houseboat on Norris Lake. My grandfather's service in Korea was a point of pride for our family and a source of lasting friendships for him. As I watched my grandfather go to work, which in Didi's case was always multiple jobs, host family, take care of aging parents, and support his kids as they started families of their own, there was a sense of urgency and responsibility that I attribute to the years he spent away from us.

"When my mom first asked me to write something from my perspective for this book, my mind kept returning to the topic of sacrifice. I am not sure when I first learned that one of Didi's jobs in Korea was to retrieve the bodies of fallen soldiers or that he missed the birth of his son, but I do know that I did not really understand the trauma he must have felt until I was an adult with children of my own. If you talk to him, he will freely tell you that he chose the 'administrative job' specifically to keep him out of harm's way so that he could get home to Mimi and Lloyd. He also speaks with pride about using his per diem to buy cigarettes, which he would sell at a profit so he could buy Christmas presents for his family back home. What he didn't tell you is that the hearing damage he sustained never recovered or that he never really got over missing the birth of his son. He also will not tell you that the war likely took from him his last night of peaceful sleep. Those sacrifices are as real today as they were back then.

"The rest of this book is his place to share his stories directly. For my part, I just want the reader to know that these are not just memories that live in the past. My grandfather's experience in the war colored everything in his life after he returned home and is a debt that cannot be repaid.

"I am forever grateful to have him in my life and will try my best to learn from the sacrifices that he made for all of us" (*Kelly Brooks*).

Proud of Didi

Lloyd Exclusive

"Before the Korean War, Dad was a dreamer but was always very shy. He had often said that he barely looked people in the eye or "past their shoes." He was an introvert who was sometimes adopted by extroverts. For example, a teacher got him involved with the drama club in high school and encouraged him to register for college courses. This young person is far different from the man I grew up with, and I believe the Korean War is a large part of this change.

"Dad quickly became a sergeant in the military, and he found that he was always in charge somewhat over young men just like himself. He had to work with obstacles and make decisions on others' behalf. When he came home, he was the only one in his family with a formal education, and so many important decisions were brought to him. I believe his time at war gave him the skills and the confidence to organize just about anything.

"Dad was able to get his degree from the University of Tennessee (UT) with a GI bill. Even with this financial support for his courses, he still had to work around the clock to take care of his family and home. After graduation, he worked as physical director at the YMCA and was the SCUBA (Self-Contained Underwater Breathing Apparatus) commissioner.

"As a dreamer, Dad had many business ventures. The only thing that held him back were friends turned into business partners who didn't have his same drive. He would end up taking on the work himself. It reminds me of stories from the war where he would take up work from fellow soldiers who were struggling without any need for recognition. The goal was just to get the job done so everyone could get home. He brought this mentality home with him. Sometimes these ventures would work and sometimes not, but he never stopped dreaming.

"One dream that kept coming to the surface was SCUBA diving education. He started a sport-diving certification program. He awarded a paper certificate he prepared. After a period of time, the YMCA generated a certification card. In the early 1960s, Dad ran a dive center called Tennessee Divers Supply with a friend for a time.

"Dad started a dive club called East Tennessee Divers Association, and it ran for years. He even had a dive tank he could put divers in for exhibits in different areas. This club was around for years to keep divers active in diving. In 1971–72 Dad opened another dive center called C/I Underwater Activities. In the beginning, Dad did this as a dive center/gun repair shop combination. He and another friend ventured out in this. He kept this business running while also working full-time at UT. I was able to see firsthand how he did whatever was needed, even when jobs were meant to be done my someone else. I learned quite a bit about business from him during this time.

"Dad left UT in his fifties to pursue his dream of teaching scuba, setting up scuba programs at UT, and coordinating dive adventures. This is why he had so many numerous travels. He also coordinated some very successful film festivals. Dad seemed to enjoy this and was very successful at it. He was a superb planner and thought through every possible issue. It was wonderful to see his talent for planning take him to so many wonderful places.

"Dad has been very successful, and until this day he is known all over the diving industry. This was really discovered when I went to the DEMA (Divers Equipment Manufacturers Association) conference and people would see my name and ask if I was Harold's son. While not every avenue panned out for him, he persevered and now has a strong legacy within the diving community. He has also inspired my son to take on SCUBA education.

"Learning more about Dad's time during the Korean War has helped me see how he became the person he is today. Some of his skills and personality came from before the war. He has always been a dreamer and had a strong sense of family, but being thrown into a leadership position across the world at such a young age brought out a confidence that I think has served him well . . . and we are better off for it" (**Lloyd Maples**).

Father and son, Lloyd Maples and airman Josh Maples

September 22, 1953, was my son's birthday. As I tried to get home to see him and his mom, I took comfort in knowing that he was safe in her loving arms and getting all her love and care. This filled me with some peace once again. I would have some catching up to do.

Lloyd

My firstborn son, I've yet to meet
Missing the beginning of his life,
From his tiny hands to his little feet
Cared for by my amazing wife.

Will I be a good father?
Give him the life he deserves?
Day by day working the plan,
I will do what I can.

His mom and I will love and protect him,
Try to provide for his every need,
In the hope that one day,
He will become the man he wants to be.

My son may have a son of his own,
And understand how it feels.
The pride and joy of being a Father,
Family together.

No idea I would make it home on Father's Day,
I find my son asleep,
Phyllis said, "You wake him up, he will be
up all day,"
Couldn't wait, I did it anyway.

Holding my son in my arms for the first time,
Mesmerized by his smile,
So full of life, his eyes they shine,
So glad I can stay awhile.
—*Karen Maples Sams 02/14/22*

Phyllis Maples

Letter to Harold Maples from Vern Ruben

July 24, 2014

Harold,

I was reading the *Graybeards* Korean War Veterans magazine in the May–June copy. Your article was most interesting to me, especially when I came to the paragraph on page 54 that started with, "The month of July always brings back a flood of memories to me," which brings back memories to me also.

I enlisted in the Minnesota Army National Guard in April 1947. In December 1950, we were notified that we would be mobilized on January 16, 1951, due to the Korean War. We would be sent to Camp Rucker, Alabama, for additional training. So, my high school girlfriend and I decided to get married on January 5, 1951, and she would accompany me to Alabama. While at Rucker, I received orders for duty in Korea in August 1951.

167

In September 1952, I arrived home to my loving wife, Phyllis. Our nine-month-old son, Gary, had been born December 22, 1951, while I was in Korea. Just thought I had to mention this to you. In Korea I was assigned at First Sergeant Service Battery, 38th Field Artillery B 2nd Infantry Division.

Vern Ruben

Response Letter to Vern Ruben from Harold Maples

Vern,

Thanks for the follow-up on the *Graybeards* article. It seems as if we had some parallel memories, which were keyed by the month of July.

You may be interested to know that I received a response as to the name of the GI referred to in the article. In fact, the veteran responding was on detail with the KIA, and I have found additional data on the person and perhaps some of the family members. I hope to do a follow-up article on the story if I can discover sufficient and valid information. It has been amazing to receive responses from several veterans who were in the division or who just wrote to reminisce; some have sent photos along with comments.

I arrived home from Korea on Father's Day. You probably, like me, did not know what to do or how to handle a newborn; quite a learning curve. Gary would perhaps say, "Dad, you did all right!"

Regards to you and your family. It was great to hear from you. We will try to stay in touch over the miles. Time is slipping by!

From one veteran to another,
Harold Maples

Letter to Harold Maples from Lynn Hahn

Dear Mr. Maples,

I read your contribution "The Mementoes Weren't All Memories" with special interest because you were assigned to a Graves Registration (GR) in your 224th Infantry Regiment. You stated you didn't have the benefit of GR training. How strange the military sometimes works. I appreciate your telling of the young casualty and what might have been had he had a flak jacket.

I was drafted on January 3, 1952, and ended up taking basic training and having GR training at Fort Lee, Virginia. I ended up arriving in Korea on August 9, 1952, and was assigned to the 148th Graves Registration Company, 23rd Quartermaster Group. The 148th Company headquarters was located in Wonju and supported the central and eastern zones of the fighting front that, by that time, had stabilized to fighting over mountains.

I was involved in search and recovery for a brief period and later ended up in operation at headquarters. The current deceased were transferred from the front with assistance from two of our platoons located near the front. They were then trucked to Wonju for fingerprinting, if possible, confirming personal effects, dog tags, and preparing for storage of the bodies in refrigeration. When there were enough remains to make a plane load, they were flown to Kokura, Japan, where positive identification was performed, embalming, casketing, and [they were] made ready for their return to the United States.

I was blessed several years ago to meet Lynnita Brown, a historian who has developed the *Korean War Educator*. She has interviewed many Korean War veterans, and the interviews can be read on her website. I spent about two years communicating with her to develop my experience of service in the army and a review of some of my life. Should you be interested, you can review the memoir in the *Korean War Educator*.

Thanks again for your memories,
Mr. Lynn Hahn

Response Letter to Lynn Hahn from Harold Maples

Lynn,

Thanks for your response. I have had calls and emails regarding the article. These comments are greatly appreciated. One response in particular came from a veteran who knew the soldier, which is amazing that the person was only on line for less than two days. The response was that they were a detail of three when the casualty happened. The KIA was Robert Walker Bernier of "I" Company, 3rd Battalion.

The response also sent a photo of a parade field where they had erected a memorial sign in Robert's honor. I thought I knew the soldier's name but was reluctant to use it in the article. I didn't want to produce an error and/or scars for a family.

My research is recovering some information on family, and so forth, so with permission I hope to do a follow-up article as well as recognition of those like yourself who provided comments.

After the ceasefire, I was TDY to Wonju for S&R with the 293rd Quarter Master Graves, 8th Army on August 2, 1953. I returned to the 224th in December 1953 in Chorwon Valley. Our S&R grids were not a great success.

Harold Maples

Quilt of Valor

The Quilt of Valor Foundation thanked veterans for their service and sacrifice on January 25, 2017, with a beautiful Stars and Stripes Quilt of Valor. This quilt was given to Harold and Phyllis was quilted by Beth Hocken Smith of Knoxville, Tennessee.

Guy was presented with the Quilt of Honor, Respect and Valor from the Greene County Quilter's Group. "I am married to my lovely wife, Ola Mae. We have been together for many wonderful years. I can't imagine my life without her by my side every step of the way. Family is so important, and I am truly blessed" (***Guy Metcalf***).

Phyllis and Harold Quilt of Valor

Guy and Ola Mae Quilt of Valor

CHAPTER VIII

LEGACY

**My view of efforts by the Korean War Legacy
Foundation to Remember the "Forgotten War"**

Phyllis has been by my side through thick and thin,
loving and supporting my every move. We have been
fortunate to attend many veteran events sponsored by the
Korean Organization. We stand in awe of the Korean people's expression of thankfulness. I have watched programs
under the Korean War Legacy Foundation (KWLF) grow
over time. This was possible in part because the growth has
been so extraordinarily rapid, thanks to the hard work of Dr.
Jongwoo Han and his many volunteers.

Phyllis and Harold—Washington, DC, July 2015

My introduction to KWLF was in the year 2012 when Dr. Han worked with several veterans in New York to collect interviews of Korean War veterans. He had a vision to capture video and artifacts to preserve the legacy of our efforts. He also wanted to show gratitude for the Korean people for our sacrifice in a way that was accessible to all. The digital platform highlights this important agenda and points to the intense growth of South Korea as a technological force. After becoming one of the largest economies in the world, the South Korean people continue to remember the sacrifice of the United States and the United Nations. The KWLF is a strong reminder of this.

Ironically enough, my introduction to Dr. Han's efforts came from a *Graybeards* magazine article. He was calling for grandchildren of Korean War veterans to join for a summit. I responded by writing to Dr. Han because it seemed that many grandchildren would be older than the requirements for the summit. He answered that age was not a factor, and so I encouraged my granddaughter Samantha Fraser to join. Samantha attended the youth summit that occurred in conjunction with the annual KWVA meeting. Phyllis and I also attended. It was wonderful to see the young people sitting with us veterans.

From 2012 to now, this organization has grown by leaps and bounds. At that time, KWLF did not have any official employees; it does have many volunteers and contract workers who manage a variety of projects that ensure our legacy will carry on.

Family members Phyllis, Karen, Samantha, and I attended a conference in Orlando, Florida. I observed first-hand the impact of the KWLF Organization. The two-day workshop created workspace for an exceptional group of classroom teachers who have shown a keen desire to teach about the Korean War and its legacy. Several groups with separate agendas worked toward a common goal. One group of highly qualified teachers is exclusively writing high-level lesson plans that connect students with primary sources from the Korean War and beyond. They have already published a book of lessons for AP world history teachers through the National Council for Social Studies. Now they turn their sights to the courses.

Another group worked specifically on the veteran interviews to isolate compelling clips that could be used in the classroom. All of their work is made available for free on the website www.koreanwarlegacy.org, where it focuses on veterans' stories. Anyone can now read interesting chapters about the Korean War and watch clips from real veterans that go hand in hand with the content. I was able to watch the hard work that goes into making this possible.

The Ambassador group designed presentation materials and set a schedule for sending teachers out to the many conferences across the United States in the coming year. This will help spread the word about these great resources so that our legacy can enter as many classrooms as possible. As part of this group, my granddaughter presented Dr. Han's book *Power, Place, State and Society*. Every project has the same goal: to make our legacy real and understandable to the next generation.

It was amazing to see how hard these teachers work for us. We should be inspired by their passion and encouraged to reach out to our own descendants and community members. Through the efforts of this organization, teachers in later years will promote our legacy to future generations. You never know who you might inspire to get involved. For me, it started with a *Graybeards* article. I hope that this article brings another veteran and his or her family into this worthy cause. If you know of a teacher in your family or community, please consider sharing this organization with them. The website specific to teacher lesson plans and professional development is www.worldhistoryde.org.

Spread the word to a teacher in your family or community by sharing the ongoing efforts to preserve the legacy of the Korean War for future generations. Veterans' stories, teacher lesson plans, and professional development are accessible to all. From my point of observation, the KWLF is a win-win for us. Thank you, Dr. Jongwoo Han.

"A big thank you to those veterans who bring their stories to life by their willingness to share what to most brings back painful memories. Stories and photographs are archived forever. Thank you to the family members of veterans who carry on the Korean War veterans' legacy. This ongoing dedication and determination to make a difference is admirable and important. The many stories, especially yours, bring tears to my eyes. Yearning to be more patriotic and take less for granted, our freedom! It is unimaginable what you endured. The cold, the terrain, the death, the unknown; and yet you persevered above and beyond for our country. South Korea is so prosperous now, rebuilt from ruins. Know that you and all the Korean War veterans stopped Communism" (***Karen Maples Sams***).

The month of July always brings a flood of memories to my mind, when I married, when the armistice was signed—never forgetting what our nation stands for and how we must fight to preserve our freedom.

Well into my nineties and counting, I have lived a long life—a son, a brother, a husband, a father, a grandfather, and a great-grandfather. My loving wife is on the other side of heaven, my angel who got her wings. I will see her again, in due time. For now, I am thankful and blessed to have lived. Making life worth living and finding that person to share life with makes for a world of happiness. Looking on the bright side, accepting good thoughts, and doing adventurous things helps you stay focused. Smile often so people will wonder what you are thinking. Teach yourself as if you were going to live forever. Share words in your heart that are sometimes difficult to speak. Life is like a ripple in a passing stream, drifting by, never to return. A meaningful life is to be cherished and remembered.

Sgt. Harold L. Maples

Harold and Phyllis Maples—Portland, Oregon

A Dream Come True

"Real heroes of this nation. They deserve our time, recognition, and respect." (***Samantha Fraser***).

Olympic Park, Seoul, July 26, 2016

"No big deal . . . just in Korea" (*Samantha Fraser*).

"Harold always wanted to return to Korea to see for himself how South Korea has rebuilt since the war. The war-torn terrain was unrecognizable when he left the war. Samantha also wanted to visit Korea. She wanted to see firsthand how South Korea rebuilt their country. Ironically neither Harold nor Samantha would make this trip alone. As their confidence and courage grew, so did the trust between them. They formed an unbreakable bond.

Olympic Park, Harold Maples and Samantha Fraser, July 26, 2016

"Harold returned to South Korea accompanied by his granddaughter, Samantha, a dream come true. Both traveled to Korea as a part of the Revisit Korea trip made possible as a result of the gratitude of South Koreans. Filled with pride for each other, they stepped off the plane onto Korean soil ready to live out their dream . . . together" (***Karen Maples Sams***).

"No big deal . . . just in Korea. Hotel map or Didi's original . . . which one to use?" (***Samantha Fraser***).

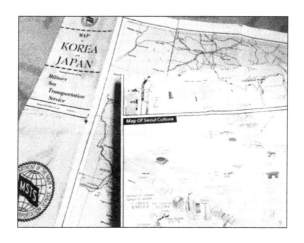

Maps of Korea

On July 23, 2016, I traveled with my Military Sea Transportation Service Map of Korea and Japan that I had during the war. My granddaughter traveled with a newer version.

"To travel with my grandfather to South Korea was an experience I will never forget. We worked for several years to get to the point where we could travel, and during that time, I learned a great deal about how much he gave to the Korean people and his fellow soldiers. I also learned about the state of South Korea after the war. One of the most striking moments was on our ride to the hotel. He was taken aback by the size and number of bridges across the Han River. He kept saying, 'This was all mud. There was only one bridge.'

"I also enjoyed seeing him thrive as a traveler. He has always been a globetrotter and an avid photographer. He was in his element in this new place. Where others might stress over not knowing the language or directions, he flourished. I got a sense of who he might have been back in the

Korean War as a young, adventurous man. I feel honored that he allowed me to join him on this trip to South Korea, an unforgettable experience" (**_Samantha Fraser, July 23, 2016_**).

Korean Flag and Traditional Attire

Samantha and I were allowed to wear cultural Korean attire. We celebrated the traditions that have stood the test of time. We saw a traditional demonstration of how Korean children and adults bow for celebrations.

Cultural experience arranged for us!

Bowing Etiquette

Samantha and I celebrated Armistice Day overlooking the Han River in South Korea. The amazing transition that unfolds is seeing the growing efforts of South Korea recovering from ashes and destruction and to see up close a booming economy. Thanks to all for your efforts in arranging the revisit for my granddaughter Samantha and me—an effort that will not escape our memories. My military unit was on the front line the day of the ceasefire. Being here on July 27 many years later and attending the cessation of hostile action ceremony at Olympic Park was very special. Unification of the two Koreas continues to be a goal.

What It Means to Return to South Korea After 63 years

The tour of the National Memorial in South Korea in the year 2016 was beyond amazing. This would be an indescribable trip with my granddaughter, the return trip of a lifetime. A veteran's revisit to a free and prosperous South Korea, standing as a result of selfless sacrifice. We remember the horrors of war and the defense of democracy and freedom.

Harold and Samantha overlooking the Han River

As I somberly remember my war experience and the many lives lost, the broken bodies I recovered, I proudly lay flowers at the base of the National Memorial in South Korea in honor of Charles Lloyd Nix and William Brady Hatton Jr. The Veteran Memorial Tablets are in the Corridor of Honor bearing all the soldiers' names who fell in the line of duty during the Korean War. "Private Nix was inducted into the army on November 5, 1951, and sailed from Seattle, Washington, on July 14, 1952, arriving in Korea on August 15, 1952. He was with the 279th Regiment Army, 279th Infantry Division for just a little over a month. He was killed in action on September 22, 1952, in the Punch Bowl, fighting the enemy in North Korea."[10] Charles was a 1951 graduate of Powell High School (PHS), where he was

---

[10] http://www.koreanwar.org/html/21962/korean-war-project-tennessee-us

a star on the Powell High School football team. We worked at the same company and attended the same church.

"PFC William Brady Hatton Jr. was with the 38th Infantry Regiment Army, 2nd Infantry Division. He was killed in action on May 19, 1951, in the battle zone of Bunker Hill located in South Korea."[11] He also graduated from PHS.

I had no idea that Charles Nix and Brady Hatton would get special recognition for their service later. They, along with three other Korean War veterans, were honored with a monument located near the American flag at PHS in Powell, Tennessee. A total of thirteen PHS students who died in the war were honored.

The names of those killed include two in World War II: Vernon Harris and Eugene Harris; five in Korea: Brady Hatton, Charles Nix, Jack Amyx, Robert Buckner, and Paul Reed; and six in Vietnam: Charles Reed, Larry Barnard, Lennis Gentry, Ray Hankins, David Marine, and Tommy Higdon.

Powell graduates KIA memorial

---

11 http://www.koreanwar.org/html/12566/korean-war-project-tennessee-us

Harold Maples laying flowers—National Memorial—selfless sacrifice

Words cannot express how thankful we were for the opportunity to return to South Korea as a part of the Veteran Revisit Program. As I stood on the rim of the Punch Bowl, my hopes were that this book, in some way, would honor soldiers who died on the field of battle, a memorial to the fallen.

Dr. Jongwoo Han and Harold Maples—revisit to South Korea, July 26, 2016

Held at the South Korean National Cemetery, we were honored to attend a ceremony so the South Korean and American Soldiers "could meet each other again." How ironic that, in the year 2016, the South and North Korean leaders were shaking hands at the demilitarized zone. Many Korean families have renewed hope that one day they can be reunited with their parents and siblings separated by a line since the Korean War. Now, South Korea ranks near the top of the most economically advanced nations in the world. Its development as a modern nation is due to the many unsung veterans who fought a treacherous ground war for democracy.

Meeting each other again

"The DMZ (demilitarized zone) tour and the laying of flowers at the National Memorial are two moments that were both full of solemn tension. Harold Maples is the most photogenic person ever" (***Samantha Fraser***—*August 3rd, 2016*).

Reminiscent and Appreciative Letter for My grand-daughter Samantha

Hey Samantha,

Enclosed is a little info and a down payment on the revisit expenses. I know what the airfare amount was, but not sure of the insurance, so I took a guess. I will never be able to repay you and your mom for covering all of the bases. Just know I appreciate all of your efforts in making the July 2016 Korea Revisit Trip of a lifetime possible. Mike was a great contributor, and I appreciate all of his efforts also. I know that you had other out-of-pocket expenses, and I want to share my part, so please don't hold out! Thanks again for everything. Love you guys bunches and Mimi does too! Didi

Harold Maples

Samantha Fraser and Harold Maples, Seoul, Korea

P.R.I.D.E.

P. for Pride, Prisoner, and Patriot
R. for Rifle, Rounds, and Rescue
I. for Injuries, Intense, and Insurgent
D. for Death, Danger, and Duty
E. for Enlist, Enemy, and Explosion (***Karen Maples Sams***)

"November 11, 2017, Happy Veterans Day, Dad. Mom held down the home front for our family while you were at war. She truly is amazing! The distance between you both only made your love for one another that much stronger. As I watch the two of you now with your outpouring of love for each other, it fills my heart. The morals and values you and Mom have instilled will last a lifetime. You are an integral part of my upbringing. As your daughter, I am so very proud of you both. So glad you got to return to Korea and see firsthand how beneficial the Korean War was. Thanks to those who, like you, never hesitated to fight for freedom. You should make another trip. Thank you for your service. Love you from my heart," **_Karen Maples Sams_** **_(Sissy)_**

Korean Revisit Trip—demilitarized zone

Arirang

"It is believed that the song "Arirang" originated from Jeongseon, Gangwon Province. Ambiguous in meaning, some linguists have hypothesized that 'Ari' meant beautiful and 'rang' referred to beloved one or bridegroom. Arirang meant 'my beloved one.' Two versions of this story exist. In the first one, the bachelor cannot cross the Auraji to meet the maiden because the water is too high, so they sing a song to express their sorrow. In the second version, the bachelor attempts to cross the Auraji and drowns, the sorrowful song is sung after he dies. The word _arirang_ itself is nonsensical and does not have a precise meaning in Korean. The lyrics of the song vary from version to version. The themes of sorrow, separation, reunion, and love appear in most. More than 600 years old, the song is sung today in South Korea, and represents the symbol of unity in the region that is divided by the Korean War."[12]

Arirang, arirang, arariyo . . .

You are going over Arirang hill.
My love, you are leaving me,
Your feet will be sore before you go ten ri.
Just as there are many stars in the clear sky,
There are also many dreams in our heart.
There, over there that mountain is Baekdu Mountain,
Where, even in the middle of winter days, flowers bloom.

Arirang, arirang, arariyo . . .
Airirang gogaero neomeoganda.
Nareul beorigo gasineun nimeun,
Simnido motgaseo balbyeongnanda.

Cheongcheonhaneuren janbyeoldo manko,
Urine gaseumen huimangdo manta.
Jeogi jeo sani baekdusaniraji,
Dongji seotdaredo kkonman pinda.

Remember all the soldiers who willingly served and did not return, the price they paid so that we could be a part of future generations with our sons and daughters, our grandchildren.

---

[12] https://en.m.wikipedia.org/wiki/Arirang

"Without Them, We Would Not Be Here"

Knoxville remembers with a memorial monument for Korean War Veterans at the Tennessee Veteran's Cemetery in Knoxville, Tennessee. This is the first memorial in Tennessee for Korean Veterans that was solely purchased, shipped, erected and unveiled by Koreans of the Knoxville Family Korean Association. The monument symbolizes the ultimate sacrifice of freedom. The membership consists of one thousand plus Korean family members living in Knoxville. The unveiling was witnessed by a crowd of five hundred–plus people and dignitaries on Monday, May 26th, 2003.

Knoxville Remembers

Knoxville Memorial—Johnny Jones, Harold Maples and Albert Clemmer

"FREEDOM IS NOT FREE" is inscribed in both English and Korean on the monument. The monument is seven feet tall, weighing two tons of black marble. The marble came from a South Korean quarry located near the Demilitarized Zone. Dr. Tom Kim, a local medical doctor and past President of the local Knoxville Association was the man who worked tirelessly to get the monument to Tennessee, located at 9901 Lyons View Place in Knoxville.

Dr. Tom Kim provided a medical clinic to local citizens in the surrounding Knoxville community at a cost they could afford. The clinic was staffed by dedicated volunteers like Joyce Keck Rasar, my sister-in-law. She gave her time in the clinic helping with the tasks at hand. Joyce was presented with a medal from the Korean War Commemoration Committee. Dr Kim spent many countless hours to keep the clinic open.

Joyce Rasar and Dr. Kim

Dr. Kim and I, along with four family members, attended Knoxville's dedication and unveiling of the Korean War Memorial. The event was attended by many local Korean War veterans. We were proud to have our wives standing by our side. Dr. Kim was a young Korean boy from North Korea who, along with his mother, grandmother, brothers, and sisters, fled from North Korea to South Korea during the campaign. War was all around them!

Local Korean restaurant, Host—Guy and Ola Mae Metcalf, Joyce Rasar, Harold Maples, Hwa Kim, and Phyllis Maples

A meaningful dedication comment: "Without them [veterans], we would not be here" (***Dr. Tom Kim***).

Under clear skies and a sunny day, the keynote speakers included Dong Yern Kim, South Korean Consulate General; United States Representative John J. Duncan Jr.; Knox County Mayor, Mike Ragsdale, and Sunny Park. Thirty-four veterans were presented with medals from the Korean War Commemoration Committee.

"As a child I saw what war can do to a nation. I saw so many dead bodies. They are in a better place, and they are with us today" (***Sunny Park***).

"We cherish the memories of each individual who collectively made up the number of dead found in jungles, beaches, fields, and oceans throughout the world" (***Lieutenant Colonel Don Amburn***).

"Memorial days are not just for picnics and barbecues—this is a historic day. We honor and respect and love you, the Korean War veterans. Thank you, Harold L. Maples, for your letter and photos" (***Dr. Tom Kim***).

Family picnic in DC

The benediction was held at the Korean War Memorial by the minister of the Korean church. The event was to "honor those who fought the good fight and finished the course" (***Reverend Dan Park***).

Veterans attended Knoxville, Tennessee memorial

Washington, DC Korean War Memorial Dedication

Our 40th president of the United States, Ronald Reagan, put together an advisory board of twelve highly decorated Korean War veterans to coordinate all aspects of the Washington, DC, Korean War Memorial's construction.

"Public Law 99–572: October 28, 1986, authorized a memorial to honor members of the United States armed forces who served in the Korean War, particularly those who were killed in action and who are still listed as missing in action or were held as prisoners of war. Congress approved the site for the memorial on September 16, 1988. The memorial is located in Washington, DC's West Potomac Park, southeast of the Lincoln Memorial and just south of the reflecting pool on the National Mall. After a national competition on June 1, 1989, a design was selected form a group of architects from the State College in Pennsylvania. The design received final approval in May 1990. The Army

Corps of Engineers officially selected the firm of Cooper-Lecky to be the architect of record. Louis Nelson Associates etched the mural in the wall, and Frank Gaylord became the principal sculptor of the Memorial statues.

"The intermingled images of the memorial recall the unity and patriotism of those who served. A sculptural column of battle-clad ground troops marches up a slope toward an American flag. Nearby is a grove of linden trees encircling a reflecting pool. At the south edge of the memorial is a polished granite wall depicting hundreds of faces of those who supported the troops: airmen, chaplains, nurses, sailors, artillerymen, and others" (***Unnamed Korean War veteran***).

Daughter laying flowers at the DC Korean War Memorial—July 2015

Phyllis and I were able to attend the dedication of the memorial from July 26 through July 29, 1995. The memorial dedication provided the platform for noting that the Korean War is no longer the Forgotten War. Hundreds of Korean

War veterans and their families were there to remember and share the dedication to fallen comrades.

A Pusan tent city was set up on the National Mall to enhance the celebration. We took a shuttle bus from J. W. Marriott Hotel located at Pennsylvania Avenue on July 27, 1995, to the dedication. We viewed the monument and the nineteen sculpted soldiers depicted in combat gear trudging wearily up the hill as on patrol. Inscribed on the memorial, "Our Nation Honors Her Sons and Daughters Who Answered the Call to Defend a Country They Did Not Know and a People They Had Never Met."

There was a 3:00 p.m. dedication for the remembrance of a military conflict that was not originally called a war by the United States. Tell that to the guys in the trenches and those laboring under combat fatigue and taken as prisoners of war. This was a bloody three-year conflict! Memories of war provoke the remembrance of those who gave their lives. We honor the heroes of freedom by the dedication of this monument. Finally, the veterans of a "Forgotten War" got their memorial.

The monument opened up at 4:00 p.m. to the public, and we hiked back at that time and met the sculptor, Frank, who designed the statues of soldiers. He was an army paratrooper in World War II from Barr, Vermont, according to the *Times Argus* newspaper. Forty-two years after the ceasefire, the memorial was dedicated by President Bill Clinton and Republic of Korea President Kim Young-sam on an extremely hot day, July 27, 2016. Medical treatment and water were available for possible heat exhaustion.

The Korean War Monument is breathtaking, especially at night. Approximately seven feet tall, each stainless-steel statue is an ominous depiction of life-like soldiers. Nineteen fighting men on a winter patrol, exhausted and frightened, trudging through the snow-covered terrain of Korea with their weapons ready for battle. You feel the cold and hardship they endured. You can see into their eyes. Destined to be the most visited memorial in the park, this leads every viewer down a trail of remembrance—a devotion of how precious freedom and peace continue to be.

Guy Metcalf, Korean War Memorial, DC

"The Korean War Memorial is very impressive, bringing you back to what war really was like from 1950 to 1953. The sun was disappearing, and the long shadows dramatized the site. Larger-than-life-size soldiers on patrol in a place of great danger. Very quiet and solemn, with no laughter or joking around. There was a large group of Asians visiting the memorial, and they were very kind to the veterans" (***Dennis Hultgren***).

Just for the record, President William "Bill" Jefferson Clinton and Vice President Albert "Al" Gore had a White House state dinner for an invited list of 180-plus dignitaries.

Needless to say, one often wonders why none of the grunts made the guest list?

A thirty-seven-cent stamp honors the fiftieth anniversary of the armistice that created the demilitarized zone stalemate between North and South Korea. This stamp recognizes the bravery of Korean War veterans and the importance of the Korean War in the United States and in world history. The first day of issue for the Korean War veterans memorial stamp was on July 27, 2003.

**First day of issue for the Korean War veterans memorial stamp—
July 27, 2003**

1985 Korean veteran stamp

What Does Memorial Day Mean to Us?

Memorial Day is a national holiday to remember our country's fallen war heroes. Always on the last Monday in May, flags are flown at half-mast and taps is played. People go to parades. My young great-grandson visited the Georgia National Cemetery in Canton, Georgia, on Memorial Day 2017 to lay flowers and remember those who have served. Family members show honor and respect to the war veterans who have paid with their lives the price for our freedom. It is a gentle reminder to our children lest they forget to pay much deserved respect to those who served. This is an opportunity to teach the younger generation the true meaning of Memorial Day. A piece of wisdom to pass along to the youth of today: Appreciate the United States and what we have. Avoid distractions now common with hi-tech communications, and be thankful.

Memorial Day

Always remember the veterans with reverence and thank God that these servicemen and women made the sacrifice across generations. As time moves on, Memorial Day loses its significance and becomes a holiday of cookouts, outings, sports events, and retail auto sales. The single most important thing to remember is why Memorial Day was established. Historically, Memorial Day was designated in 1968 by the United States Congress, making May 31 a United States holiday.

The three-day holiday uprooted the real meaning of Memorial Day, except for what is being nurtured by a few families across the USA! Sadly, the real reason for Memorial Day is succumbing to a lack of interest. Remembering the fallen should be the rallying call of observance. We look forward to this weekend. I think we have everything we need: hamburgers, hot dogs, buns, potato chips, ketchup, mustard, and drinks. Anything else? Oh yes! Our veterans!

Family picnic

My story would not be complete if I did not include a personal writing about my lifelong soulmate, Phyllis. A person who always helped me pay it forward, a loving wife and mother, grandmother, and great-grandmother. With a smile on her face, she added the coating to our many happy family experiences. I am beyond thankful for her love and support. May you read her words and see that her life is equal to mine, and her presence made our family complete.

My Soulmate, Phyllis

"My name is Phyllis Eleanor Keck, and I was born February 17, 1932, in Knoxville, Tennessee, I was delivered at home to my parents, Sherman and Bernice Keck, by Dr. Parker. The doctor, who lived about a mile away, practiced medicine from his home, which was at the corner of Inskip Road and Coster Avenue. Our home was on Gregory Street, which was a rock road, and it dead-ended before reaching Clinton Highway. Gregory Street later was made West Inskip Drive and was cut through to Clinton Highway.

"Hazel Bernice Lay Keck was my mother, a stay-at-home mom and a descendant from Ireland. She was called Johnny by her family. My father, Phillip Sherman Keck, was a descendant from Germany. They were married July 4, 1921. They already had two children before I was born, named Sherman Blake and Winifred Joyce. My brother Blake was about ten years older and Joyce was about five years older. My father, Sherman, was a barber who had a shop on Depot Street a few doors below Southern Depot in Knoxville. This was close to the railroad tracks on South Central Avenue and a few blocks from downtown Knoxville.

"I visited Dad's shop and Bill Long's Bar several times. The bar was right next door. No one from the bar ever bothered me since they knew that Dad would be on their case if they did. When I was old enough, I would walk from the barbershop to downtown Knoxville to the movies or for shopping at the various stores. I would go on the sidewalks in front the Southern Depot or sometimes would go on South Central, which was shorter but a rough neighborhood. I liked the musical movies better than the others—my favorite was *State Fair*. A friend of mine, Coy Zirkle, took me to a mystery movie at the Tennessee Theatre that scared me half to death. It showed a man's eye who was hiding in women's closets and attacking the women to kill them. I also attended the Rivera Theatre and the Bijou some as well. The Bijou Theatre had a segment on Saturday morning where anyone could participate in singing or playing an instrument. Several of my friends attended this and participated, but I never did get to go because Mother said I had to stay at home and help clean the house.

"Blake, Joyce, and I didn't have toys as such while growing up. We played tag and hide and go seek, climbed trees, and caught butterflies and put them in glass jars. We caught June bugs and tied strings around their legs and let them fly around. We played in the woods around us, and I got poison ivy all over me. I had a few dolls that I left outside in the rain, and they got ruined; I never played with them much. We did other outside things to keep us busy.

"Dad always brought home a box of fruit (apples, oranges, and nuts) for our Christmas. I can remember the first Christmas present I ever received was a watch that my father gave to me, which I thought was the greatest thing that had ever happened to me. Mother was a little bit lazy and required Joyce and me to help her with the housework and the cooking when we were old enough. She cleaned house on Wednesday while we were in school, and we had to finish most of the jobs when we got home. Then she cleaned again on Saturday. Joyce and I cleaned while Mother talked on the phone. She did the washing, but we did the ironing. We didn't have water in the house when we were younger, and we carried water from a well that was behind us in the alley. I had a few fights with a neighborhood girl over the water pump because when I started to the pump for water, she always would run ahead to beat me. I pulled her hair really good one day, and she then stopped trying to beat me. We finally got water in the house and an inside bathroom that really made us very happy. The boys in the neighborhood decided to turn the outhouse over one Halloween, but Dad was waiting for them and made them put it back where it was supposed to be.

"When I was a little older, I cut paper dolls and colored in coloring books a lot—this was always a good indoor activity for me. I also collected movie star photos from books and magazines. The first bicycle that Joyce and I had was an old blue bike with one handle broken off completely. I don't remember where we got this bike. I finally got a good bike and rode it all over the community.

"When I was a child, one of my jobs was gathering eggs from the henhouse. Mother sent me out after the eggs, and I stretched and reached them but got chicken mites all over the front of me and my clothes, itching to high heaven. Another incident was when Sandy decided to gather the eggs, and she got chicken mites all over her too. Mother told me to clean her up, which was a big job! I never liked chickens again!

"My grandmother, Lydia Ola Kitts Lay Wallace (Mother's mother), lived in East Knoxville near Chilhowee Park, and we would visit her often. She sewed Joyce's and my dresses every summer for us to start school. We stayed with her about a week for her to do this. Mother bought the material and thread. I never knew my grandfather, William Milton Lay, since he and Grandma were divorced when I was very small. We visited the Chilhowee Park when the TVA Fair was in session early in September and would stay until after the fireworks were over at night. This was always lots of fun for us.

"I walked from home to Inskip Elementary School for eight years, then rode a school bus to Central High School for four years, graduating in 1950. I never wanted to drive a car, so when I turned sixteen years of age I couldn't drive, and it didn't even bother me a bit. My boyfriend, Harold, asked Dad to borrow his car, and he took me on a driving run. We drove around a while, and I cleaned out a ditch; I didn't do very well. He decided to take me to the Tennessee Department of Safety and take the license exam, which I did. Believe it or not, I passed the test and got my license. When we showed it to Dad, he just about passed out; he couldn't believe it!

"Joyce looked after me while I was growing up and took me everywhere she went when I was younger. I'm sure I was a pain in the neck during those times. I was very active at Bookwalter United Brethren Church, taking part in their plays and other holiday programs. Christmas plays were always a big deal for me. I acted as an angel in the Christmas pageant. We always received a bag of candy and fruit at

Christmas that I was really proud to get. Evelyn Jean Starnes and I sang duets for the services, and I sang solos sometimes.

"Harold never did own a car, nor did his family, but he would borrow a truck from Jake Armstrong to come and see me. We would go to the drive-in theater on Clinton Highway, and his friend Calvin Gentry would get in the bed of the truck and watch the movie while we stayed in the front seat. Sometimes we would ride with someone else on a double date.

"Harold and I used to ride with Jack Ward to the mountains after church turned out on Sunday afternoons. We really had some fun times. One day we were wading in a mountain stream, and I tripped and fell into the water with my dark blue crepe dress on. We left directly from my church, so I had no change of clothes. Harold was getting ready to go back to school and had his suitcase with him. I wore a pair of his jeans and a T-shirt and made do until I got back home.

"We attended Bookwalter United Brethren Church on Central Avenue Pike; later it became Bookwalter Evangelical United Brethren and then Bookwalter United Methodist. Dad would go with us to church on Sunday mornings but never went at night. I grew up attending this church. I met Harold when I was sixteen, and he joined the Bookwalter Church after we started dating.

"After graduating from Central High, I began Knoxville Business College in downtown Knoxville along with one of my friends, Mary Lynn Thomas Skeen, for about six months. This was all new to me since I had no training in typing, shorthand, or business practices. I worked really hard and learned to type pretty well, but my shorthand wasn't too good. I took the Tennessee Valley Authority (TVA) test twice before I passed it. Jake Armstrong asked me if I would work at the Knoxville YMCA, so I quit business college and started working there at $25.00 a week. This was money I never had before, and I really enjoyed the work. My brother Blake kept bugging Arlene Snure at TVA to hire me. Arlene finally did arrange an interview for me, and I got a job with TVA in the steno pool. I liked it okay and liked the salary even better. Harold attended Tennessee Polytechnic Institute in Cookeville, Tennessee, while we were dating and then the University of Tennessee (UT) after we married. He bought us a small home in Maryville, Tennessee, located on Pennsylvania Avenue behind Broadway Baptist Church. He was working at Fulton-Sylphon while attending classes. He got his draft notice in September. Soon after we were married, he left for the United States Army in October 1952, and he was in Korea for twenty-one months.

"He came home for good in June 1954 to our nine-month-old son, Harold Lloyd Maples Jr. Lloyd was asleep early in the morning when Harold got home, and he wanted to wake him. I told him if he woke him, he wouldn't go back to sleep until that night, but he woke him anyway. And sure enough, Lloyd was awake all day. Lloyd usually went to sleep about 7:00 at night and woke up very early in the morning.

"After discharge from the Korean War, Harold went back to school, leaving in the mornings around 6:00 a.m. He paid for his education with financial assistance, the GI Bill, and working full-time. After receiving his diploma, he quit work at Fulton-Sylphon, and he took a job with the YMCA in Knoxville for a long time. He got his bachelor of science degree in health education from UT and almost got his master's degree in educational guidance but quit school before he finished his master's. He had intentions of completing his schooling to get the degree but got too involved with working full-time and other things. He never completed his master's degree.

"I stayed home with Lloyd until I went to work at the East Tennessee Tuberculosis Hospital in Knoxville when Lloyd was fifteen months old. I worked as a secretary there until Karen Ann was born on January 24, 1956. I stayed home with the children until Karen was about eighteen months old before I took a job working in the office at the UT Memorial Hospital. I then moved in a couple of weeks to TVA and stayed until I retired in 1986.

"Harold, Jim, and Buddy Clark built a houseboat at Cherokee Lake in Jefferson City, and our families spent lots of time waterskiing, swimming, fishing, and all the good stuff you do while at the lake. We spent almost every weekend on the houseboat. We worked hard throughout our lives, cutting corners where we could so we could afford to travel. Our lives were filled with adventure around every corner" (***Phyllis Keck Maples***).

Our family will always celebrate the legacy Phyllis left for us. A legacy that was so aptly applied in her favorite scripture verse was her continuous hope for her family members and her amazing act of caring:

> *Therefore, as God's chosen people, holy and dearly loved, clothe yourselves with compassion, kindness, humility, gentleness and patience. Bear with each other and forgive whatever grievances you may have against one another. Forgive as the Lord forgave*

you. And over all these virtues put on love, which binds them all together in perfect unity. (Col. 5:12–14)

Phyllis Maples—ready to travel

A Proud Man

A proud man,
I stand,
A yearning for life.

A proud man,
I seek,
Adventure over the next hill.

Searching, searching,

For untraveled lands,
Searching, searching,
For uncharted waters;
The new, the exciting awaits.

A Hunter and a Diver,
A Husband and a Father;
A Teacher and a Scholar,
A Grandfather and a Great-Grandfather;
A Korean War Veteran.
The land and sea,
They challenge me! (***Karen Maples Sams***).

Proud to be an American—Harold Maples

Phyllis

Never a complaint, your needs came
before hers,
Always helping others;
A genuine belief that everything works out
for the best,
Blessed.

A life of faith and a strong love of family,
Always a sweet and gracious lady;
Lifting you up in her silent prayers,
Silent tears.

Lasting friends and memories;
Scripture carried her through the years.
(***Karen Maples Sams***).

Love is when two hearts find a happy place beside
each other.

Walking hand in hand

God offers this hope: "I am certain that God, who began a good work within you, will continue his work until it is finally finished on the day when Christ Jesus returns" (Phil. 1:6, http://www.biblegateway.com).

In other words, whatever journey God begins in your life and heart, he promises to finish—in his perfect timing.

In Loving Memory of Phyllis K. Maples

February 17, 1932–June 19, 2018

"Please pass the following along and be proud of the country we live in and those who serve to protect our 'GOD-GIVEN' rights and freedoms. I hope you take the time to read this . . . To understand what the flag-draped coffin really means . . .

"The Meaning of the flag-draped coffin will help you understand. The flag that laid upon the coffin and is surrendered to so many widows and widowers. Do you know that at military funerals, the 21-gun salute stands for the sum of the numbers in the year 1776?

"Have you ever noticed that the honor guard pays meticulous attention to correctly folding the United States of America Flag 13 times? Some think it symbolizes the original 13 colonies. It is much more than pomp and circumstance. Each of the 13 folds holds special meaning. We learn something new every day!" (*Graybeards* **Magazine**)

Old Glory

Folds of Honor and the Meaning of the Flag-Draped Coffin

- The 1st fold of the flag is a symbol of life.

- The 2nd fold is a symbol of the belief of eternal life.

- The 3rd fold is made in honor and remembrance of the veterans departing the ranks who gave a portion of their lives for the defense of the country to attain peace throughout the world.

- The 4th fold represents the weaker nature, for as American citizens trusting in God, it is to Him we turn in times of peace as well as in time of war for His divine guidance.

- The 5th fold is a tribute to the country, for in the words of Stephen Decatur, 'Our Country, in dealing with other countries, may she always be right; but it is still our country, right or wrong.'

- The 6th fold is for where people's hearts lie. It is with their heart that they pledge allegiance to the flag of the United States of America, and the Republic for which it stands, one Nation under God, indivisible, with Liberty and Justice for all.

After the flag is completely folded and tucked in, it takes on the appearance of a cocked hat, ever reminding us of the soldiers who served under General George Washington, and the Sailors and marines who served under Captain John Paul Jones, who were followed by their comrades and shipmates in the Armed Forces of the United States, preserving for them the rights, privileges and freedoms they enjoy today.

- The 7th fold is a tribute to its Armed Forces, for it is through the Armed Forces that they protect their country and their flag.

- The 8th fold is a tribute to the one who entered into the valley of the shadow of death, that we might see the light of day.

- The 9th fold is a tribute to womanhood, and mothers. For it has been through their faith, their love, loyalty and devotion that the character of the men and women who have made this country great has been molded.

- The 10th fold is tribute to the father, for he, too, has given his sons and daughters for the defense of their country since they were first born.

- The 11th fold represents the lower portion of the seal of King David and King Solomon and glorifies in the Hebrews eyes the God of Abraham, Isaac and Jacob.

- The 12th fold represents an emblem of eternity and glorifies in the Christians eyes, God the Father, the Son and Holy Spirit.

- The 13th fold, or when the flag is completely folded, the stars are uppermost reminding them of their Nation's motto, 'In God We Trust.

Father and daughter

General Bradley's Message

"As your commander, I proudly salute you, the American soldier, the finest in the world. May your service with the Sunburst Division in Korea ever be a solemn reminder of the obligation that is every American's, that of defending the priceless heritage that has been handed down to us by the American soldier of another day. May we always have the faith and courage to defend that heritage. God Bless you all" (***General William. J. Bradley***).

During the Korean conflict, the 40th Division was a National Guard activated from the state of California and received additional training in Japan before entering the conflict. The guardsmen rotated home after their tour of duty and were replaced by enlisted, regular soldiers, I being one of them.

The official name for the 40th symbol was Sunshine or Sunburst. Early guardsmen took some ribbing for being from a National Guard outfit. The ribbing resulted in an unofficial name, succumbing to regular army soldiers' sense of humor.

40th Infantry Division's Class A patch

What I think others should know about the Korean War

I think the Korean War could have been won, but President Truman feared Russia might enter the conflict. General Douglas McArthur, the designated commander, executed a full-scale invasion of North Korea. If this invasion had been allowed to continue, it might have been successful. Later, Truman removed MacArthur and replaced him.

How much is known about the Korean War? During
the war, television and press made little mention as to what
actually happened. Your immediate family may have known.
When you came back home from the war, others would ask,
"Where have you been? I haven't seen you in a while. Has it
been two years, three years?" They felt no pain from it back
in the States. It was not like World War II, when everyone
was on the same page.

Efforts have been made to incorporate the history of
the Korean War into public schools. An example is what
Samantha, my granddaughter, has done with the Korean
War Legacy Organization and history classes. History of the
Korean War is left to a paragraph or two in a history book, if
that. They want to leave out what happened. Students learn
what they are taught, what is in the curriculum. The Tell-
America and the Korea War Veterans Association do a good
job of going to the local schools and educating the students
about what occurred. Veterans tell their stories and share their
war experience. This sharing could be a thing of the past.
Continuing to interview Korean War veterans is the one thing
I see that brings the information to the forefront. Information
is archived and made readily available. Maybe this will be
momentum for positive happenings in the future.

Battle of the Outposts

The Korean people are the exception; they still recognize the importance of the war and are so grateful to veterans. Many South Koreans do recognize what their freedom means. South Korea is a booming economy now of hardy workers— that entire peninsula. It is amazing to me how much the give-back is from South Korea, more so than from Americans. South Koreans recognize what the United States did for their country in the Korean War. They celebrate and honor Korean War veterans multiple times each year and recognize that

Americans fought for their freedom and democracy. China prefers the buffer provided by the demilitarized zone.

North and South Korea run their countries very differently: communist rule in North Korea versus a democracy in South Korea. Could we move the no-man's land up closer to the North Korea and China border, allowing the North and South Koreans to unite with one another, especially at the family level? The many refugees could create a safe haven. Why not? It's going to cost you either way.

Words of advice for any generation are to remember Old Glory and keep it flying. Whatever it takes to do it? Sacrifice extends throughout many years, and if you are not knowledgeable of those sacrifices, then you don't know what it costs both mentally and physically. So when the youth of today pick up their cell phones, iPads, and laptops, encourage them to stop and think how that was accomplished. Search for personal information, goals, and assistance, and you will probably find some personal help from it. Realize that freedom has never been free.

The history of the Korean War is left to a paragraph or two in a history book, reflecting an intentional attempt at leaving out what happened during the war. Students learn what they are taught in their history class, what is in the curriculum. Now there are few veterans remaining to tell their stories and share their war experiences.

It's still the greatest country in the world. We have a lot of problems. They seem to be magnified, but the young people can solve these problems if they choose. Military action has never solved too much. World War II was supposed to end it. We haven't won one since.

Five things I took home from the war: honor, humility, sacrifice, importance of family, and a stronger faith. "O beautiful for spacious skies, for amber waves of grain, for purple mountain majesties above the fruited plain! America, America, God shed His grace on thee and crowned thy good with brotherhood from sea to shining sea."

Write It Down—Harold Maples

A publication circulated free by the Republic of Korea under the title *Korea Reborn . . . A Grateful Nation* is a book that honors war veterans and the country's exceptional growth. At best, it summarized that from the ashes of a war-torn country rises a prosperous nation due to veterans who sacrificed on their behalf. Peace, friendship, and prosperity are indeed to be cherished.

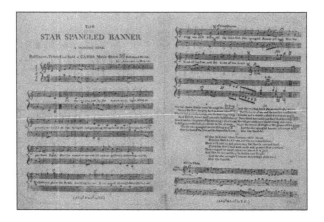

Star-Spangled Banner

**Appreciation event in honor of American Veterans of the Korean War—
your names are beating within the heart of our land—Phyllis and
Harold Maples**

ADDITIONAL PHOTOS

George Campbell from Ohio

DeRenzo from New York

Fred Ellick

Thanksgiving Day—Harold Maples, Ed McMullen

Harold Maples and Lieutenant Wilfred E. Smith

Lieutenant Wilfred Smith

Keith Daily, Howard Hinkle, and Harold Maples

George Campbell, Bruce Johnson, Gene Schock, and Ed McMullen

Harold's selfie

Harold with Chinese carbine

Harold Maples and soldiers

Harold Maples, Guy Metcalf, and Robert Singer

Camp Drake, Japan, Prov Co 569 and field house

Guy Metcalf and weapon

Guy Metcalf and Harold Maples—Korean weapon

Guy Metcalf and Harold Maples

Harold Maples and Lieutenant Smith

Guy Metcalf

Lee and recovery team

Lee and search and recovery

Lynn Hahn

Unknown soldier in village

Unknown soldier

Tank and unknown soldier

Mama-sans doing washing

Papa-san zipper repair, Wonju '53

Yong Dung Po '53—Hinkle

Korean children

Korean villagers

Quick exit—Wonju

Han River—Seoul

Day trip to Hiroshima for training and visitation

**Small boy in elaborate clothing riding on horseback in the parade—
Hiroshima, Japan, April 10, 1953**

Image176.pdf
Korean War Memorial

Korean War Memorial

Korean War Memorial statue

Memorial Star and Korean War Memorial

Korean War Memorial—Karen Sams

Marilyn Monroe

Phyllis and Harold Maples—Powell Station

ACKNOWLEDGMENTS

- My wife, Phyllis, my love, my heart, she stood by my side through it all, never faltering, never losing faith.

- My parents, William Matthew and Myrtle Bell Maples, facing adversity and a hard life to provide for our family.

- Our children: son, Lloyd, and our daughter, Karen; being parents fills our hearts with pride

- Our amazing grandchildren: Kelly, Samantha, and Josh; being grandparents gives us joy beyond words.

- Our great-grandchildren: Madeleine Reece, David Benjamin, Sylvia Clay, Henry Jackson, and Katelyn Mary; our hearts are full.

- My sisters, Leona and Margaret; sisterly love, so many memories.

- My sister-in-law, Joyce; a heart of gold, a lifetime of helping others.

- Support from my peers.

Writing a book is more difficult than I could imagine—turning ideas into stories. Karen and her mom spent countless hours aiding in the production of this personal account. I am eternally grateful for their efforts. The completion of this writing would not have been possible without their relentless effort and the contribution of the persons mentioned above. Hopefully as individuals read these pages, they will become kindred with the folks who brought this story to life—a story featuring family legacy through meaningful life experiences.

References

Battle of Kapyong: http://en.m.wikipedia.org/wiki/Battle_of_Kapyong

Bible Verse: A Time for Every Deed: Ecclesiastes 3:2–8 New Revised Standard Version (NRSV) Ecclesiastes Bible Verses http://www.biblegateway.com

Bible Verse: Colossians 5:12–14, Bible Gateway http://www.biblegateway.com

Bible Verse: John 3:16 https://en.wikipedia.org/wiki/John_3:16

Bowing Etiquette: Bowing—https://en.wikipedia.org/wiki/Etiquette_in_South_Korea

Combat Infantry Badge (CIB): https://en.wikipedia.org/wiki/Combat_Infantryman_Badge.

Dennis Hultgren: Dennis gave the author written permission to use his photos in this book. Picture was taken at the Punch Bowl, To Korea and Back Home Again, page 79.

Flag of the National League of Families POW/MIA Flag:
—https://en.wikipedia.org/wiki/National_League_of_Families_POW/MIA_Flag. .

General William Weigel: https://en.m.wikipedia.org/wiki/USS_General_William_Weigel_(AP-119)

Robert Louis Stevenson: No Room for Cowards.

Graybeards **Magazine**: The Reminisce—Dennis E. Hultgren.

Graybeards **Magazine:** Knoxville Remembers, Harold L. Maples, page 60.

Graybeards **Magazine:** One veteran's view of efforts by Korean War Legacy Foundation to remember the 'Forgotten War' , Harold Maples, 40th Infantry Division, 224th Regiment

Graybeards **Magazine Online**: Korea Veterans—The *Graybeards* Magazine is the official publication of the Korean War Veterans Association https://kwva.us/?page=arch_graybeards.

Graybeards **Magazine:** The Missing Flac Jacket, Harold L. Maples.

Guy Metcalf: Guy gave the author permission to use his photos and story in this book.

Harold Maples and Phyllis Keck's Wedding Announcement: Knoxville News Sentinel, Knoxville, Tennessee, July 12, 1952.

Honoring All Veterans: Opinion Editorial *Knoxville News Sentinel*, Sunday July 28, 2013, 2F. Author Unknown.

Kapyong High School: The Fireball Publication of the 40th Infantry Division, APO 6, Corporal Robert McLean, May 16, 1954, Vol. 2. No. 15, page 4.

Karen Maples Sams: A Proud Man, Guard Duty, Lloyd, Phyllis, Porcelain Doll, P.R.I.D.E.

Korea Reborn . . . A Grateful Nation Honors War Veterans for 60 Years of Growth: Limited Edition Commemorative Book, Published byRemember My Service Productions, a division of StoryRock, Inc., in cooperation with Seoul Selection, copyright 2013.

Korean War Legacy Foundation (KWLF): Veteran Stories is www.koreanwarlegacy.org . Another website specific to teacher lesson plans and professional development is www.worldhistoryde.org—Dr. Jongwoo Han.

Korean War Veterans Association, Inc.: Graybeards History: https://kwva.us/?page=about_graybeards_history.

Leo Bromleny: Leo gave the author written permission to use his photos and story in this book. Worn On The 4th Of July was co-written by Harold Maples from Leo Bromleny's perspective about the Korean War. The article can be seen in its entirety in the Korean War Graybeard's July—August 2016 issue.

M1 Garand Rifle: https://en.m.wikipedia.org/wiki/M1_Garand.

Nick Spartichino: A Buddy Remembers—Nick gave the author written permission to use his photo and the photo of Bernier Field in this book, along with Nick's personal story and that of Robert W Bernier's story.

PFC Charles Lloyd Nix: Per the website, "all information of Remembrance entries is available to the public at large," http://www.koreanwar.org/html/21962/korean-war-project-tennessee-us

PFC Willliam Brady Hatton, Jr.: Per the website, "all information of Remembrance entries is available to the public at large,"—http://www.koreanwar.org/html/12566/korean-war-project-tennessee-us

Robert Frost: The Road Less Traveled https://upload.wikimedia.org/wikipedia/commons/e/e8/The_Road_Not_Taken_-_Robert_Frost.png

Robert W Bernier: Korean War Project Remembrance— https://www.koreanwar.org/html/2110/korean-war-project-massachusetts-us51214051-pvt-robert-walter-bernier

Robert Louis Stevenson: No Room for Cowards.

Song—Always: https://en.m.wikipedia.org/wiki/Always_(Irving_Berlin_song)

Song—America the Beautiful (O Beautiful for Spacious Skies): https://en.wikipedia.org/wiki/America_the_Beautiful—Written by Kathrine Lee Bates—Music composed by Samuel A. Ward, Newark, New Jersey, 1895.

Song—**Arirang:** https://en.m.wikipedia.org/wiki/Arirang.

Song—Star-Spangled Banner: The earliest surviving sheet music of "The Star-Spangled Banner," from 1814 National anthem of the United States https://upload.wikimedia.org/wikipedia/commons/7/7a/Star_Spangled_Banner_%28Carr%29_%281814%29.png

Song—The Army Goes Rolling Along: https://en.wikipedia.org/wiki/The_Army_Goes_Rolling_Along#Lyrics

Soviet Union in the Korean War: https://en.wikipedia.org/wiki/Soviet_Union_in_the_Korean_War.

The Badge of Glory: Unknown Veteran

The Battle of Bloody Ridge: en.wikipedia.org/wiki/Battle_of_Bloody_Ridge

The Korean War Educator: http://www.koreanwar-educator.org/memoirs/hahn/index.htm

The Korean War Veterans Association, Membership Directory: SGT Harold L. Maples, Sr., 2014, page 179.

The Meaning of the Flag-Draped Coffin: Credit for this Article goes to: The *Graybeards* Magazine—Ron Gorrell: Founder of the 224th Infantry Regiment Association—May to June 2018, Page 8.

The Registry of the American Soldier: Downloadable Form—https://armyhistory.org/wp-content/uploads/2016/05/registry_sign_up_sheetUPDATED.pdf.

The Road Less Traveled Definition: https://en.wikipedia.org/wiki/Wikipedia:Taking_the_road_less_traveled

Thirteen Alumni Killed in the War Memorial: https://www.knoxnews.com/story/shopper-news/halls/2022/11/11/powell-high-school-knoxville-tn-memorializes-13-alumni-killed-in-war/69638377007/

Unnamed Korean War Veteran: Combat was extremely fierce during the three years of war.

USNS *Marine Carp:* https://en.wikipedia.org/wiki/ USNS_Marine_Carp_(T-AP-199).

USS General William Weigel: http://en.wikipedia.org/wiki/ USS_General_William_Weigel_(AP-119)

Washington DC Korean War Memorial Dedication: Unnamed Veteran.

Without Them We Would Not Be Here: The *Knoxville News Sentinel*, "Always Remember," Senior writer Fred Brown, brown@knews.com, page A1 and A7, Tuesday May 27, 2003 (Dr. Tom Kim, Lieutenant Colonel Don Amburn, Reverend Dan Park).

Witness to War Interview: Martin S. Madert—martinmadert@witnesstowar.org—www.witnesstowar. org—Search Harold Maples Video—https://www.witnesstowar.org/search_result?share=68c8848183

About the Author

- Bernie Empleton YMCA SCUBA Award

- Book Credits Jacket Design

- Certified SCUBA Diving Instructor (YMCA, PADI, NAUI)

- Commercial Diver Underwater Construction

- Director of Diving Tours Worldwide

- Early Pioneer in Developing the Sport of Scuba Diving

- Front Cover [[Image01.pdf

- Knoxville Sports Hall of Fame

- KWVA Membership and Participation

- Owner of SCUBA Diving Operation—C/I Underwater Activities

- Staff Sergeant Korean War Service

- Underwater Photographer and Organizer of Diving Film Festivals

- United Methodist Church Member

- University of Tennessee, Bachelor of Science in Education

- University of Tennessee Master Study Educational Psychology

- University of Tennessee Assistant Director of Under Graduate Admission

- YMCA Physical and Aquatic Director

- YMCA Southern Area SCUBA Commissioner